HUGH

HUGH

The unofficial and unauthorised biography of
HUGH GRANT
by Dan Whitehead

Published by
Kandour Ltd
1-3 Colebrook Place
London N1 8HZ

This edition printed in 2004 for
Bookmart Limited
Registered Number 2372865
Trading as Bookmart Ltd
Blaby Road
Wigston
Leicester LE18 4SE

First published June 2004

ISBN 1–904756–16–6

Production services:
Metro Media Ltd

Author: Dan Whitehead

With thanks to: Jenny Ross, Emma Hayley,
Lee Coventry, Paula Field

Cover design: Mike Lomax
Cover Image: Rex Features

Inside Images: Rex Features

© Kandour Ltd

Printed and bound by Nørhaven Paperback, Denmark

HUGH GRANT

FOREWORD

This series of biographies is a celebration of celebrity. It features some of the world's greatest modern-day icons including movie stars, soap personalities, pop idols, comedians and sporting heroes. Each biography examines their struggles, their family background, their rise to stardom and in some cases their struggle to stay there. The books aim to shed some light on what makes a star. Why do some people succeed when others fail?

Written in a light-hearted and lively way, and coupled with the most up-to-date details on the world's favourite heroes and heroines, this series is an entertaining read for anyone interested in the world of celebrity. Discover all about their career highlights – what was the defining moment to propel them into superstardom? No story about fame is without its ups and downs. We reveal the emotional rollercoaster ride that many of these stars have been on to stay at the top. Read all about your most adored personalities in these riveting books.

HUGH GRANT

CONTENTS

HUGH GRANT

FACT FILE

Full name: Hugh John Mungo Grant
Eye colour: Blue
Date of birth: 9 September 1960
Place of birth: London

Height: 5' 11"
Marriages: None
Children: None

Star sign: Virgo (24 August – 23 September)
Virgos are typically cautious and methodical, attracted to a certain sense of order and seeking out whatever knowledge is required to put them in a position to exert control over their environment. This attention to detail can result in slightly obsessive behaviour and a tendency to view life in a cynical fashion. Their fastidiousness often leads Virgos to great success, but is balanced out by a natural modesty and desire to deflect praise. Other famous Virgos include D.H. Lawrence, Peter Sellers and Mickey Mouse!

HUGH GRANT

Chinese birth sign: The Rat

Those born in the Year of the Rat are both experimental and adaptable, traits that often manifest in a broad entrepreneurial streak. They believe in making their own luck, and are possessed of a natural sobriety and passion that helps them achieve this goal. These tendencies can become excessive, suggesting an addictive personality, although their open-minded communicative nature helps keep them balanced with the help of loved ones.

Career high:

Convincing the makers of Four Weddings and a Funeral that he wasn't too good looking for the role of dithering Charles led to Hugh's blockbuster breakthrough in 1994, and international fame. The movie was the most successful British movie ever made at the time.

1

Introduction

HUGH GRANT

INTRODUCTION

He's the Oxford fellow who stumbled into acting, the middle-class son of a carpet salesman who became famous for bumbling around stately homes and posh weddings, the megastar actor who claims he doesn't like acting, but has appeared in over 40 movies and TV shows.

On screen he's romanced a glittering array of Hollywood's hottest actresses, and tackled medical conspiracies, the mafia and a giant white worm. Off screen he's hogged the headlines with his high profile girlfriend and her safety pin dress, as well as finding lifelong notoriety after a little Divine intervention in Los Angeles.

HUGH GRANT

INTRODUCTION

Hugh Grant is Britain's biggest movie star, an actor whose talent for comedy has often been misjudged by those who assume he simply plays himself. He's starred in movies that have made nearly a quarter of a billion dollars, and yet he got his first screen credit in a posh student film about...posh students.

From bit parts in a Nottingham theatre, through comedy revues at the Edinburgh Fringe, and on to the top of the box office charts, Hugh has remained constant – charming, witty and ever so slightly sarcastic, obsessed with perfection and performance while winking to his audience as if to say, "This is all awfully silly, isn't it?"

He is Britain's leading bona-fide movie star, and this is his story...

2

Class act

HUGH GRANT

CLASS ACT

Despite the infamous plummy accent and upper class image, Hugh Grant was born into the resolutely middle-class world of Chiswick on 9 September 1960. The second son of James, an office carpet salesman, and Fynvola, a primary school teacher, it was a completely normal and stable childhood, unfolding in a suburban backwater of London where the genteel pace of life insulated its inhabitants from the tumultuous world outside.

The social revolutions rocking the world as the Sixties carved their way through history made little impact on Chiswick, and Hugh spent his formative years dwelling on his boyish obsession

CLASS ACT

with football, playing (and fighting) with his older brother, also named James, a veritable army of Scottish cousins (courtesy of his mother's side of the family) and absorbing the varied activities arranged by his parents. While some branches of the Grant clan prospered, Hugh's family were at the mercy of the economic tide, and the life of a carpet salesman in the economically turbulent 60s and 70s was a precarious one. Though they were never destitute, neither could James Sr afford to abandon his uninspiring sales career to indulge his true passions – including watercolour painting and amateur sports.

"A lot of people end up in jobs that aren't perhaps their absolute, true calling," Hugh revealed in an interview many years later. "But they still commit all their energies to it, and become quite adept. My father was in carpets for years. He didn't really love carpets, but he became pretty good at flogging them!"

Instead James and Fynvola channelled their aspirations into their children, instilling in them knowledge and love of literature, history, theatre and the arts. Television was discouraged in favour of museums, outdoor sports and reading – everything from Boy's Own annuals to P.G.

CLASS ACT

Wodehouse. Despite the relentless modernisation of sixties life, Hugh's cultured and polite upbringing owed much to his parents belief in the values of decades past.

The only intrusion of modern life's more grim facets came in the form of a nearby doctor who, it was alleged by the local gossips, had murdered his wife and scattered parts of her body around Chiswick. Hugh's mother would hear nothing of it, and insisted that Hugh and James always treat the man with civility and respect should they meet him in the park.

"She was so convinced that he was innocent that she made me and my brother, who was quite young at the time, be especially nice to him," Hugh recalled to host Jay Leno on The Tonight Show. "So we used to say good morning and good evening. We went round and helped him do his shopping one Christmas. We painted his fence." The good doctor turned out to be guilty and was convicted of murder. "There's a corner of me that still thinks he's a nice man because mum said so," laughed Hugh.

Though as a child Hugh was already confident and handsome, with a quick and sometimes caustic wit inherited from his mother,

CLASS ACT

he showed little affinity with acting or performing in his day to day life. He'd choose a football and a muddy field over any dabbling in the arts every time. Indeed, if it weren't for the school gates that fate pushed him through at the age of eight, acting may never have played a part in Hugh's life at all.

Latymer Upper School was founded in 1642 on the posthumous instruction of Edward Latymer. The school was created on land bequeathed in Latymer's will, on the banks of the Thames, to cater for the education and well being of poor boys from the Hammersmith area. Such a long history inevitably meant that by the time Hugh embarked on his education there, tradition and commerce had long since overshadowed the altruistic nature of the school's founding but, even so, Latymer remained outside of the introverted circle of the more famous public schools, and was open to the brightest offspring of the area, regardless of income. Though it would only begin admitting girls in 2003, Latymer was – and is – a fairly forward-looking school for its vintage. Educational innovation and a culture of encouragement and self-sufficiency were in marked contrast to the public schools, with their matrons, arcane rules and straw-boater uniforms.

HUGH GRANT

CLASS ACT

This peculiar mix of centuries-old tradition, where 'masters' would mentor their young charges, and modern liberal attitudes that would be frowned upon in the hallowed hallways of Eton meant that Old Latymerians (or Old Lats as the school lingo calls them) often followed different career paths than the graduates of similar establishments. While other schools sent forth their students to become captains of industry, sportsmen or politicians, Latymer school leavers were just as likely to be drawn to literature, academia and the arts.

In 1976, as Hugh collided head-on with the world of adolescence, Latymer made the final switch from state grammar school to independence. Parents could no longer rely on the local education authority picking up the fees for talented pupils, and the establishment went through a shift in image as far as kids and parents were concerned, and what had been one of the most desirable grammar schools in the area, suddenly became a wannabe upstart competing for wealthy students against more established private schools. Caught between two stools in Britain's increasingly garbled class system, the school's dilemma reflected Hugh's own mixed background – appearing very

CLASS ACT

posh from one side, and yet never quite posh enough from the other.

Hugh had inherited his clipped accent from his mother's precise speech, but even though his good humour and passion for sports made him popular, there was still snobbery and teasing. Having a father who sold carpets made Hugh an easy target for jibes, as did his delicate good looks and floppy fringe.

"I wasn't happy as a teenager at all", Hugh told an interviewer, "especially with my hair. When I went on French exchanges, all the locals would call me 'Mademoiselle', and I never completely got over that."

It was under these circumstances that Hugh turned his sharp tongue to his advantage, and was quite adept at giving as good as he got, deflecting insults with self-deprecating wit and a politely barbed comeback.

The drama societies during Hugh's time at Latymer were made up of a strict hierarchy, based on the make-up of genuine medieval dramatic guilds. At the time of Hugh's education, drama fell under the auspices of Colin Turner, the Middle School English Master, and the sort of inspirational tutor made famous by stories such

CLASS ACT

as *Goodbye Mr Chips* and *Dead Poets Society*. Quick-witted and fiercely intelligent, Turner took great pleasure in overturning some of the more stuffy notions about literature and the arts, demanding that drama should be as compulsory as English lessons, and that a love of words and performance enhanced all areas of intellect and life. Alan Rickman, another great British actor who would later co-star with Hugh in *Love Actually*, was but one of many Latymerians to benefit from Colin Turner's enthusiastic encouragement.

The bright and lively Hugh relished life as a Journeyman (the youngest ranking of the drama societies), taking to this open-minded and stimulating environment like a duck to water and, with his dry wit, became one of the leading lights of this small enclave. He soon became one of Turner's favoured pupils, a regular at the tutor's informal extra-curricular get togethers where the tall and well-spoken academic would regale his young wards with opinions on the London stage, the arts and movies. Far from having the seriousness of drama forced upon them, being a Journeyman meant having fun, improvising skits and taking pleasure in exploring their imagination. This was in direct contrast to the

CLASS ACT

nearby Corona stage school, whose pupils would often mingle with Latymer's during the hometime rush to the Ravenscourt Park tube station. Though Latymer's pupils were encouraged to seek auditions for plays and films (one of Hugh's fellow students, Dominic Guard, appeared as the lead in *The Go-Between* with Julie Christie and Alan Bates while at school) there was a thinly veiled resentment between the two sets of students – with Corona's openly flamboyant "look at me" dancers and actors being viewed as hopelessly pretentious by the more earthy Latymerians. Hugh has retained this distaste for the showy and insincere side of showbusiness ever since.

"The British theatre has a whole language of its own," he told CNN in 1999. "Everyone's a luvvy. Alright luvvy? How are you feeling? How's Mrs Tummy? The whole thing makes you want to throw up."

Hugh's first shot at leading man status came on the back of a change in Latymer tradition. It was usual for the school's dramatic productions to draw from all the years, with the plum roles reserved for the older students, and the bit parts and behind the scenes work divided between those lower down the hierarchy. In 1975

CLASS ACT

the rules changed, and Hugh's year was to put on a show all of their own, with no senior pupils to take the best roles. Not only that, but it was to be a co-production with Godolphin Girls School, meaning that the female roles would actually be played by real females! This was especially good news for Hugh, who had already suffered endless abuse for his cross-dressing turn as one of the Von Trapp daughters in the schools all-male version of *The Sound of Music*.

The play chosen was the 1851 French farce *The Italian Straw Hat*, a typically ribald and silly parade of misunderstandings, mistaken identities and frantic chases around the scenery. The male lead, Fadinard, is a flustered bridegroom who finds his perfect wedding plans falling apart after his horse eats a woman's straw hat and she demands he replace it. The part was perfect for Hugh, always more interested in light-hearted laughs and romantic froth than the weightier end of the dramatic spectrum, and he won the role with ease. Despite the play being a rather obscure affair, and one not highly regarded in theatrical circles, Hugh nonetheless went out of his way to find a performance of it and study it, to better educate himself on the demands of the

CLASS ACT

play, and – crucially – how to make it funny. This strange mix of laid-back nonchalance followed by intense perfectionism has typified Hugh's approach to his movie career ever since.

The play was as big a success as a school play can be, and Hugh found himself with his first taste of fame. He received glowing reviews, and was interviewed for the school paper and enjoyed the attention of female cast members drawn to the warm glow of his popularity.

More roles followed in a succession of school performances (though he lost out on the lead in Romeo and Juliet to his older brother, himself one of the schools most popular sixth formers) and as Hugh moved up through the school years, he graduated from Journeyman to full-blown member of the Gild, the highest echelon of Latymer's dramatic ladder.

However, as well as his dramatic success Hugh was excelling academically and was a model pupil. Writing for the school paper, he was infamous for his extravagant purple prose when reporting on cricket matches, and even interviewed his English Master, Colin Turner, on the importance of drama.

In 1978, as one of Latymer's brightest and

CLASS ACT

most multi-talented pupils, Hugh was awarded a scholarship to Oxford University to read English. It was to be a move which would cement his love of performance, and his desperation with the nonsense that can surround it.

3

Man about Oxford

HUGH GRANT

MAN ABOUT OXFORD

Before embarking on the next stage of his education, Hugh spent his post A-Level summer travelling through Italy in the company of a girlfriend plucked from Godolphin Girl's School. When she returned home, Hugh carried on alone – though he swapped their villa accommodation for the more frugal world of youth hostels. With his wanderlust satisfied, he headed home to begin life at Oxford University's renowned New College in the autumn of 1979.

It was in the rarefied atmosphere of this famous seat of learning that Hugh finally found a social setting that matched his own maturing

MAN ABOUT OXFORD

tastes and personality. As the Eighties dawned, Britain was undergoing a seismic shift in mood and culture. After the rebellion of the Sixties and the strife of the Seventies, this new decade cast aside the hippies and punks and embraced wealth and status, with new Prime Minister Margaret Thatcher leading the charge. For an aspirational middle class teenager starting at one of the most privileged universities in the world, it was a predictably heady time.

His scholarship earned Hugh a preferential place in the Oxbridge social circle, with access to the best accommodation and parties. Hugh took it all in his stride, applying himself equally to his studies and his social life, joining many of Oxford's student societies and hosting drinks and tea parties like a latter day Noel Coward. He flitted between libraries, tennis courts and extravagant formal balls with the aplomb of somebody who had been waiting for this lifestyle to come around.

Despite his dramatic successes at Latymer, Hugh wasn't taken with the theatrical environment of Oxford. There was a brief flurry of excitement in the town when director Michael Cimino came to town to shoot scenes for his follow-up to *The Deer Hunter*, the famously disastrous western *Heaven's*

MAN ABOUT OXFORD

Gate, but Hugh wasn't seduced back into acting by the brief flutter of Hollywood glamour. Despite a plethora of acting companies at the University, both stuffily official and endearingly amateur, having gone from top of the heap at school to one of the crowd at Oxford, Hugh found it too much effort to begin climbing the ladder again. Although during his first year, he did take part in a university production of *Twelfth Night* that toured France, in the small role of the servant Fabian. After spending the spring of 1980 sharing the homes of French families with histrionic undergraduate egos, he returned to England and concentrated on his studies and his partygoing instead.

Hugh loved the social whirl of Oxford life, and as so many fellow Latymerians had also won places in the University's varied colleges, he arrived with a ready made network of old friends. His confidence and Byronic good looks soon meant that he was one of his year's most sought after party guests, and his membership of high-minded drinks clubs like the Boojums Society (taking its name from Lewis Carroll's *The Hunting of the Snark*) and the innocently-titled Keats Society formed a central part of his outgoing lifestyle.

HUGH GRANT

MAN ABOUT OXFORD

More notoriously, Hugh was an enthusiastic member of the secretive Piers Gaveston Society. A brash and snotty recent addition to Oxford's roster of student groups, having been founded in only 1976 when most had their origins in the 1800s, the Piers Gaveston Society took its name from Edward II's executed confidante and alleged lover, who famously met his demise on the wrong end of a red-hot poker. The Society embraced the legend of this character, his reportedly stinging witticisms, his lampooning of courtiers (the Society was nothing if not a punk-inspired kick against Oxford's stuffy regimes) and his attention-grabbing dress sense. Camp flamboyance was the name of the game, fancy dress, outrageous behaviour and utterly hedonistic excess was their aim. Despite the homosexual overtones of the society's credo (their club crest features a rather perky male organ), the all-male members were largely upper-middle class straight men who enjoyed rowdy drinking and eating with a deliberately esoteric attitude. Certainly, their parties and meetings were infamous for their rotation of venues – few Oxford establishments allowed them back a second time – and for their bawdy behaviour.

Membership came only via invitation –

usually engraved and slipped under the recruit's door – and it came with a seventy pound price tag. Despite his affectations, Hugh remained a middle-class boy and had no family wealth to fall back on. Despite this, he realised that being a Gaveston would open up vital doors within Oxford society. Their assured arrogance, lewd wordplay and romanticised hell raising appealed to his sense of humour, and he dipped into his dwindling grant money for the membership fee. Like all new members, he started out as a Minion, reporting to one of the senior Gavestons – who went by florid titles such as Master of Debaucheries, Warden of the Closet or Keeper of the Plumes – with the aim of inheriting their mantle when they graduated.

In among these impossibly privileged young men, Hugh was drawn most to Danny Daggenhurst, a member of the University boxing team and an incredibly bright scholar to boot. Danny was the son of a Greek diplomat, and it was his fathers wish that he become a Daggenhurst rather than a Karamanos in order to grease the wheels of Oxford's insular social engine. Hugh and Danny became great friends, both possibly recognising in the other a fellow interloper in this head-spinning new world of booze, girls and eyeliner. Despite the often-sordid Gaveston events and parties, Hugh remained shrewdly distanced from the deeper excesses to which others subjected themselves. He sidestepped the buffet of narcotics available on campus, and never let the outrageousness of the night interfere with his academic work during daylight hours.

Though he had chosen the hedonistic clique of the Gavestons over Oxford's many dramatic societies, as his second year of university life rolled along, fate was conspiring to push young Hugh in front of the cameras for the first time. While Hugh was making a name for himself as a rakishly charming social aesthete, another student was also becoming a fixture around the University, though for quite different reasons. Mike Hoffman was an American student, studying at Oxford after winning one of the highly prized Rhodes Scholarships, of which only twenty were available each year. Hoffman found the arch pomposity of Oxford life both entrancing and hilarious, and could often be seen stalking the leafy quadrangles with his camera, always ready to engage fellow students in typically enthusiastic American conversation. He was planning to make a film about modern Oxford student life, the notion of these wealthy young men and women wilfully adopting (and adapting to) an old fashioned *Brideshead Revisited* lifestyle tickled his creative impulses, and he wanted to capture it in more than mere still photography.

Luckily, the Oscar-winning director John Schlesinger, helmer of such classics as *Midnight Cowboy* and *Marathon Man*, was also a graduate of the same Oxford college that Hoffman was studying at. The Provost of the college arranged for Schlesinger to read Hoffman's proposed movie (co-written, with one Jeremy Beadle), and the heavyweight director liked what he saw. The script, entitled *Chameleon*, was a suitably operatic tale of doomed lovers torn asunder in the shadow of those hallowed Oxford spires. Ironically, Schlesinger had himself made a very similar amateur movie during his time at the university and agreed to consult on the project. With a genuine Hollywood legend involved in the project, the acting fraternity at Oxford was buzzing with excitement at the idea of a real movie, rather than predictable old stage work. Hoffman had a very clear idea of the sort of people he wanted to see in his movie, however, and that didn't include the self-consciously dramatic members of Oxford's theatre elite. The movie was about beautiful people living exquisite-yet-hollow lives, and when Hugh auditioned (along with seemingly every other undergraduate) Hoffman knew he'd found the ideal actor for the pivotal role of Lord Adrian.

Hoffman drew on the student population to make his movie (which had ballooned from a short into a full-blown feature), getting music students and local bands to supply the soundtrack, while badgering businesses into offering up their services in exchange for a sliver of reflected glory when the movie was complete. The Gaveston Society even made use of their own unique talents, supplying enough roaringly drunk extras to make the film's party scenes reek of authenticity. With a budget of £30,000 raised from friends and family, Hoffman was ready to go.

John Schlesinger was a man of his word and took the time to attend the 35 day shoot, ran workshops for the cast and crew and, while he offered advice, he was gentlemanly enough to allow Hoffman to make the movie his own way. Throughout the shoot, Hugh maintained an air of jocular amusement – often voicing his dismay at what a "twit" he appeared – but he was intently focussed on the time spent with Schlesinger in rehearsal, and his theatrical past at Latymer gave him a professionalism that many of the student cast lacked.

The BBC bought a rough cut of the movie for £20,000 and promptly changed the title to the more marketable *Privileged*. It opened in a (very) limited cinema release in 1982 in London and New York and was roundly savaged by the critics. The hastily assembled storyline, pulled together from reams of footage, was viewed as wildly over-ambitious (contrasting a production of the tragic play *The Duchess of Malfi* with the real life trials of its well-to-do student heroes) and the acting was stiff and parodic. Hugh, credited by his then-preferred nickname Hughie Grant, wasn't spared either – his foppish Lord Adrian was considered more caricature than character.

Nevertheless, the experience of making *Privileged*, coupled with the boundless praise from Mike Hoffman and the encouragement of John Schlesinger, turned Hugh's attention back to thoughts of acting again. He excitedly auditioned for a part in *Greystoke*, a new Tarzan movie and though the part he was considered for was yet another society toff, he believed for a short time he

MAN ABOUT OXFORD

might actually be chosen as the new Lord of the Apes. He won neither part, and he returned to university life having learned an important lesson about the harsh realities of the acting profession outside of the self-contained world of academia.

Privileged had opened with Hugh already well into his final year at Oxford, and he had abandoned the on-campus luxuries for a shared house with Danny Daggenhurst instead, though their Gaveston connections meant that their student digs were a cut above the usual festering rented suburban semi-detached. Though his brush with the real world of acting had left him reeling with ideas, the time had come to justify his scholarship and knuckle down for the gruelling slog of Oxford finals. After a period of intense last-minute revision and study, Hugh left Oxford University with a respectable second-class degree. He was offered the chance to continue his studies with a PhD in Art History at the Courtaulde Institute in London, but he turned it down. His ambitions now lay elsewhere.

4

A life on the fringe

HUGH GRANT

A LIFE ON THE FRINGE

With Oxford life now ebbing away, the social circle in which Hugh had flourished for three years began to disperse. Unlike his wealthier classmates, Hugh had no trust fund or deep-pocketed parents to fall back on. While many of these friends could afford to take some time out and 'find themselves', had jobs already lined up by their network of friends and relatives, or could opt to remain in the comfortably insulated bosom of academia, finding paid work was a matter of some urgency for the 22-year-old Hugh. His elder brother James had, to the surprise of many, moved into a successful banking career following

A LIFE ON THE FRINGE

his graduation, but there was now little chance of Hugh following in such conventional footsteps. Despite his protestations about the silliness of acting and his feigned lack of interest in the craft, Hugh obviously wasn't ready to go from auditioning (albeit unsuccessfully) for Hollywood movies to working in some anonymous office in a suit and tie. Like a floppy-fringed shark sensing blood in the water, Hugh had tasted glamourous fame and wanted more.

Sadly, the reality proved rather more elusive than the dream and with no agent or Equity card to help shape a film or TV career, Hugh reluctantly took up a position with the well-respected Nottingham Playhouse repertory theatre company. From the rivalry between Latymer and Corona Stage School, and through his deliberate avoidance of Oxford's more ingrained dramatic traditions, Hugh had always kept his distance from the kiss-kiss luvvy subculture that typified theatrical folk, and now he found himself forced to throw himself into the middle of just such an environment. Throughout his amateur acting career, Hugh had been used to being at the top of cast lists, his charm and looks helping him rise through the ranks within the closed and controlled world of school and

A LIFE ON THE FRINGE

university. In the real world, things were horribly different. Hugh went from being a popular and in-demand actor to just another ambitious face, and the fall from leading man to walk-on extra was a galling one. His time at Nottingham was a frustrating and painful one. Hugh lasted a little over one season with the Nottingham Playhouse, but the experience wasn't entirely wasted. During his time there he had found a kindred spirit in Chris Laing, another jobbing actor and writer who shared Hugh's sense of humour and love of puns and impersonations. Together they began putting together short comedy sketches and enjoying the thing that gave Hugh the most pleasure on stage – making people laugh.

Eager to put Nottingham behind them, Hugh and Chris headed back to London with their burgeoning comedy routine, performed under the name The Jockeys of Norfolk – a suitably obscure reference to a line from *Richard III*. While honing their act, and attending auditions (including landing a small role in Mel Gibson's remake of *Mutiny of the Bounty* before a lack of union credentials forced him out), Hugh worked the menial job market like any struggling actor, even appearing in a photo-love story for 1984's *Secret*

A LIFE ON THE FRINGE

Love Annual as the sensitive Brian saving a girl from a loutish boyfriend.

The mid-Eighties were a good time to be part of an experimental comedy troupe in London as the "alternative comedy" scene washed away the old clichés of mother-in-law jokes and pub stand-up. Oxford and Cambridge shared a long history of producing influential and offbeat comedic talents, from the satire of Peter Cook to the anarchy of Monty Python. The Eighties were no different, as people like Stephen Fry, Griff Rhys Jones and Rowan Atkinson continued the tradition. The Jockeys of Norfolk fitted in well with this new scene and while their venues were less salubrious than the likes of rising stars Rik Mayall and Ben Elton, they began to pick up a small cult following. They were not alone in this exciting new world of comedy and they shared the circuit with, among others, a young Canadian comedian called Mike Myers, then working as a warm-up man for Timmy Mallett's Saturday morning children's shows, but would later find movie success with *Wayne's World* and *Austin Powers* amongst others.

Hugh and Chris found themselves beckoned closer to the inner circle of this new comedy culture when they began writing and producing

A LIFE ON THE FRINGE

radio commercials – in their own inimitable style – for TalkBack Productions, the production company set up by Griff Rhys Jones that, to this day, continues to foster new British comic talent. Their radio ads and Jockeys of Norfolk sketches all came from a shared love of both mocking and celebrating English stereotypes, while also carrying an undercurrent of wicked sarcasm. The Jockeys most popular piece was a recreation of the nativity performed as an Ealing comedy, with cut-glass British accents, terribly polite angels and boorish cockney shepherds. Similarly, one of their radio campaigns for Brylcreem drew on the format of the stiff 1950s BBC public service broadcasts to turn the product's outdated image into an ironic selling point.

As their fanbase grew among the backrooms of London's pub circuit the Jockeys of Norfolk decided it was time to take their routine to a larger audience, and in 1985 they set off for the Edinburgh Festival – the traditional proving ground for new comic talents. The festival was, and still is, split into two halves; one showcasing the official cultural world of new theatre and performance, and The Fringe, a free-for-all in which jugglers, comedians and anyone with a half-baked idea for a show can try to drum up an audience and a few column inches in the next morning's newspaper. According to legend, their first show saw a monumental six tickets sold.

Luckily, also at the festival was TV host Russell Harty, picking the cream of the fringe shows for exposure on his highly-rated talk show. Harty immediately warmed to Hugh, seeing star potential in this handsome young man with impeccable comic timing, and the Jockeys of Norfolk found themselves faced with a make-or-break opportunity in front of the nation. Unfortunately, sketches that had been foolproof in front of a rowdy and up-for-a-laugh pub audience fell flat in the impersonal surroundings of a TV studio, and far from being revealed as the future of British comedy, the Jockeys of Norfolk appeared as little more than enthusiastic ex-students mucking about. Their passion extinguished, the Jockeys went their separate ways.

Hugh had never given up on the dream of movie stardom that his brief brush with Tarzan had nurtured, and through perseverance, his efforts were starting to pay off. He landed a supporting role in the 1985 TV special *Jenny's War*, a sprawling three-hour transatlantic co-production

A LIFE ON THE FRINGE

based on the true life story of a woman who goes behind enemy lines in World War II to rescue her son when the army leave him for dead. Hugh's name, no longer going by the sophomoric "Hughie", was way down the cast list next to people like Jeremy Bulloch (an actor whose most famous role would be the faceless Boba Fett in the *Star Wars* movies) but it was at least a speaking part and allowed him to share the billing with respected names like Robert Hardy and Nigel Hawthorne. The TV movie was poorly received, its overly earnest plot rendering it more like a wartime soap opera than a TV event to be remembered.

Even so, Hugh had broken through and more TV roles followed – with his looks and accent almost always seeing him cast as the ineffectual toff or a stiffly repressed Lord. A minor role in Martin Shaw's dramatisation of the race to the South Pole, *The Last Place On Earth*, failed to open the doors to stardom, nor did a co-starring role in Channel 4's stuffily highbrow drama *Lord Elgin And Some Stones Of No Value*, about the controversy when Britain removed ancient sculptures from the Parthenon in order to "preserve" them. A handful of other small TV roles filled out the next few years, with supporting roles

A LIFE ON THE FRINGE

in one-off dramas, or episodes of anthology shows such as the supernatural series *Shades of Darkness*, which saw Hugh once again cast alongside Robert Hardy, as well as Miranda Richardson. It was clear that while television might provide a steady trickle of supporting roles, albeit within the restricted field of "posh fop", the leading roles proved ever elusive.

With his frightfully English persona, there was one arena where Hugh's talents fitted perfectly, and it was one he had tried to break into once already. The Merchant-Ivory production team, made up of producer Ismail Merchant and writer/director James Ivory, were rapidly becoming famous for their lush adaptations of British literary classics, and were considered a shot in the arm to the struggling British film industry (ironic given that Merchant was born in Bombay, and Ivory in California). In 1985 the pair had scored a critical and commercial hit with an adaptation of E.M. Forster's *A Room With A View*, a movie for which Hugh had auditioned unsuccessfully. They stayed with the work of Forster for their follow-up project – a film version of Maurice, the author's highly personal novel about coming to terms with homosexuality in the

A LIFE ON THE FRINGE

morally restricted world of Edwardian Britain. Forster struggled with the story – and the personal feelings it sprang from – and eventually the book was published in 1971, the year after Forster's death. Julian Sands, the actor who had shone in *A Room With A View*, was lined up for the lead role of Maurice, a Cambridge student who is coaxed into accepting his homosexuality by his extravagant friend, Clive Durham. Durham then decides that he's not gay after all, leaving poor Maurice alone and bewildered. Luckily, in a rather obvious piece of wish fulfilment from Forster, Maurice finds true love in the arms of Durham's openly gay gamekeeper, Alec.

But then, just days before filming was due to begin, Julian Sands dropped out of the lead role, and frantic recasting took place. James Wilby, a stage actor who had impressed James Ivory with his theatrical work, was moved over from a small supporting role to the lead. Hugh had auditioned, along with every other British actor it seemed, but – as with *A Room With A View* – had heard nothing back. The pivotal role of Clive Durham was actually still open, as Ivory couldn't decide between his shortlist of actors – of which Hugh was one. By sheer luck, the writer on the movie was Kit

HUGH GRANT

A LIFE ON THE FRINGE

Hesketh-Harvey, a writer and performer who had shared his dressing room with the Jockeys of Norfolk in Edinburgh. Kit gave his endorsement to James Ivory, and the director agreed – Hugh Grant would be their Clive Durham.

Filming took place over the summer of 1986, and while the relatively inexperienced Hugh found it difficult to adjust to James Ivory's famously laidback style of directing, he nevertheless managed to exude, as Merchant-Ivory's press material put it, "a blend of dead-on English public school arrogance and intimate vulnerability". The movie was a hit both with arthouse audiences and the critical establishment, with Hugh sharing the Best Actor award from the Venice Film Festival with co-star James Wilby. *Maurice* also launched the notion of Hugh Grant: Sex Symbol upon the world, with lusty fanmail pouring in from smitten female viewers as far afield as Japan, as well as an expectedly enthusiastic response from the gay community.

With an award-winning role in a highly praised movie, the film offers began to arrive more frequently. *Maurice* had seen Hugh share screen billing with highly respected thespians like Denholm Elliot, Ben Kingsley and Simon

A LIFE ON THE FRINGE

Callow, and his next project would feature an equally star-studded cast – though Hugh would only end up with eight lines. The movie was *White Mischief*, a sly look at the sexual misbehaviour of British ex-pats in Kenya during the dying days of the Empire, and it starred Greta Scaachi as the temptress whose erotic allure unbuttons the polite but depraved English society, as represented by Charles Dance, Joss Ackland and John Hurt.

Hugh's blink-and-you-miss-it turn in *White Mischief* may have been a big screen return to the supporting roles he'd so quickly grown tired of in television, but his next film would see him back in the leading man role for surely one of the strangest movies in his – or any other – filmography.

Writer, producer, actor and director Ken Russell was already regarded as the enfant terrible of British cinema by the time Hugh Grant crossed his path. A bizarre combination of refined English gentleman, with a love for opera and literature, and a peddler of shamelessly titillating exploitation, by the time Russell's career collided with Hugh in 1988, the director had already turned out such varied movies as *Women In Love*, *The Devils* and rock band The Who's rock opera,

A LIFE ON THE FRINGE

Tommy. What they all shared in common was a hallucinatory mixture of high art and low sleaze, filmed with giddy abandon by the famously extrovert Russell.

In 1986 Russell had dipped a toe in the waters of horror with *Gothic*, a typically debauched dramatisation of the events that led the creation of the novel *Frankenstein*. As poets Byron and Shelley indulge in narcotic and alcoholic excess one stormy night Shelley's lover, Mary, is pulled into their twisted games of sexual adventure and emotional ruin, forcing her to face up to her own secret fantasies and fears. Aptly titled, *Gothic* dripped with dark debauchery and evidently gave Russell a taste for the genre. So it was that he penned a very loose adaptation of Bram Stoker's obscure final novel, *The Lair of the White Worm*. Written in 1911, just one year before his death, the novel remained obscure for quite justifiable reasons – crushed by exhaustion and disease, Stoker's final work was a wildly over-the-top fable of ancient snake cults, and not the product of a writer at their peak. Nonetheless, Ken Russell saw potential in the tale and updated it to modern day Derbyshire, mixing in elements from the local legend of the Lambton Worm for good measure. In the film, a Scottish archaeology student digs up what appears to be the skull of a giant snake in the grounds of Mercy Farm, itself part of the D'Ampton estate, owned by Lord James D'Ampton, a distant descendant of a Middle Ages knight who supposedly slew a monstrous worm that terrorised the area. On this rather slender framework, Russell created a lurid and explicitly sexual yarn that also included topless nuns, Jesus Christ, boy scouts and a predatory immortal snake priestess who longs to revive her ancient snake god from its subterranean grave, played by future *LA Law* star Amanda Donohoe in various stages of undress (and confusion). It's a dizzying mish-mash of Freudian and Christian metaphor, disorientating dream sequences and surreal art movie flourishes, strained through the Hammer Horror format, before being presented as a kinky blue movie and the end result is both remarkably bad and mesmerisingly wonderful. Hugh naturally appeared as the thoroughly decent Lord James D'Ampton, a role that allowed him to inject more than a little sly humour into a now-familiar upper class character, and also gave him the chance to play a man of action, luring Donohoe's worm-goddess out of her mansion by playing snake charmer music through loudspeakers on top of his stately home, leading a local expedition into vast caves to flush the beast out and even wielding a huge broadsword to chop a possessed snakewoman into two gory pieces. Needless to say, for this and many other reasons, the movie has since become a cult favourite.

Unlike many actors who look back on early forays into cheap horror cheese with dismay, Hugh has often referred to *Lair of the White Worm* with great fondness, occasionally calling it his favourite of his movies after *Four Weddings And A Funeral*, something that confused people accustomed only to his charmingly shy turn in the smash hit comedy, but an admission that makes perfect sense when viewed in the light of his membership of the uproarious Piers Gaveston Society. Indeed, it's easy to imagine the gruesomely naughty *Lair of the White Worm* as the theme for one of the societies famously outlandish parties.

Ironically, the same year that saw the release of *Lair of the White Worm* also saw Hugh take on the role of Lord Byron in another look at the same events which had inspired Ken Russell's *Gothic* a few years earlier. *Rowing With The Wind* was a Spanish movie that followed free-spirited poets

A LIFE ON THE FRINGE

Shelley and Byron, and their respective lovers Mary and Claire Clairmont, around Europe. In the film Mary fears that her fertile imagination, responsible for the creation of Frankenstein, has cursed her and as misfortune befalls those around her, she imagines the fictional monster is the cause. The movie itself vanished without trace, failing to pick up distribution in the UK, and would have remained largely unremarkable, were it not for the fact that the part of Byron's lover, Claire, was played by a 23-year-old dancer and model called Elizabeth Hurley.

Meeting over dinner at the director's house, the sight of Elizabeth was enough to convince Hugh to commit to the movie and the pair struck up an intense friendship which soon blossomed into full-blown romance. Once filming, which took the cast all over Europe, had completed Hugh and Elizabeth's relationship endured. Even at this early stage though, the strain of balancing two showbusiness careers was something the pair had to cope with. As Hugh continued to search for a leading role that would allow him to deliver on his early promise, Elizabeth had signed on as the lead in a new Dennis Potter TV drama, *Christabel*, and it was while promoting the series in America that

A LIFE ON THE FRINGE

she decided her destiny lay in the US. She decamped to an apartment in Los Angeles, commuting back to spend time with Hugh and take part in fashion shoots, before heading back to the US to continue trying to break Hollywood.

Despite the success of *Maurice*, none of Hugh's follow up projects were successful enough to turn him into a star, and the ones that were often featured him in only small supporting roles. The sad fact was that the British film industry was in crisis during the Eighties, and only had sporadic successes. Naturally, the worthwhile roles within these movies were few and far between and there were often more actors than parts – forcing Hugh to compete with the likes of Julian Sands and Daniel Day-Lewis for the same roles.

As the Eighties gave way to the Nineties, Hugh found his career treading water, if not slowly sinking. Lead roles in stinkers like *Bengal Nights* and a supporting role in the Anthony Hopkins drama *The Dawning* may have been enough to pay the bills and fund Hugh's gregarious social life, but they really weren't advancing his career. Movie work became less frequent, and turns in soapy TV mini-series such as Judith Krantz's *Till We Meet Again* began to feature heavily. The British made bodice-ripper *Lady and the Highwayman* represented the creative lowpoint of this period. Based on a predictably gushing Barbara Cartland novel, the hugely expensive lightweight swashbuckler cast Hugh as the masked Silver Blade, a roguish highwayman who frees a woman from her loveless marriage with a swish of his sword.

Things started to pick up in 1991, with another leading role in a proper theatrical movie. *Impromptu* found Hugh back on familiar turf – a period costume drama about beautiful and talented people fumbling around affairs of the heart. In it, Hugh starred as the composer Chopin who, while attending a gala for famous writers and musicians, finds himself pursued by a doggedly determined female novelist going by the pseudonym George Sand, and who was shocking 1830s' society with her masculine wardrobe and cigar-smoking antics. More of a genteel farce using historical figures than a genuine attempt at a biography of either character, the movie received lukewarm reviews but it was enough to put Hugh back on the movie map.

He followed up on the promise of *Impromptu* by taking another lead role, this time for the controversial director Roman Polanski in *Bitter Moon*, a psychological thriller in which Hugh began his on-and-off tendency to play bashful innocents seduced by outside forces both emotional and sexual. The movie saw Hugh and Kristin Scott-Thomas as Nigel and Fiona Dobson, a British couple sailing to India via Istanbul. Peter Coyote co-starred as the wheelchair-bound Oscar, a man who slowly draws Nigel into his world of bitter revenge by regaling him with explicit confessions about his life with his dangerously seductive girlfriend Mimi. The movie was loathed by critics – "wretched excess" according to one review – but the kudos of working with a director such as Polanski just about made up for the rather stressful experience.

Hugh followed *Bitter Moon* with a return to the comfort of Merchant-Ivory, for whom he took a small role in *The Remains Of The Day*. Unlike the days of struggling in tiny roles, this was more of a favour to friends, and something quite common among the Merchant-Ivory regulars where cast and crew would frequently overlap, and help out where needed. Indeed, Helena Bonham Carter appeared in an uncredited role in

A LIFE ON THE FRINGE

Maurice, despite starring in *A Room With A View* only a few years earlier.

Up until this point, Hugh's career – and the British film industry itself – had been largely fixated on the past, with costume dramas, period biographies and literary adaptations dominating the screen. But an opportunity lay around the corner which would drag British movies back into modern times, and turn Hugh into a global superstar overnight.

5

Fame and infamy

HUGH GRANT

HITTING THE BIG TIME

T he year of 1993 would prove to be a busy, yet massively rewarding, year for Hugh. First of all, he had to jet off to the other side of the world, to Australia in fact, for shooting on John Duigan's *Sirens*, yet another movie that would require Hugh to portray the repressed Englishman abroad. The film, based on real life events, centred on Anthony Campion, an English minister who believes himself to be rather ahead of his time (the time in question being the Twenties), and his wife Estella (played by Tara Fitzgerald). They're heading for a new life, and a new flock, in Australia but the bishop asks them

HITTING THE BIG TIME

to intervene in a delicate matter first. A local artist, Norman Lindsay, is famed for his morally decadent lifestyle – sharing his home with three rarely clothed curvy muses – and one of the works in his latest exhibition, entitled *Crucified Venus*, is deemed a step too far by the Church. Campion is tasked with convincing Lindsay to withdraw the offending work from display, but both he and his wife find themselves shocked, intrigued and eventually seduced by the artist and his models' life of carefree sexuality.

The real life Norman Lindsay (portrayed in the movie by the Australian actor Sam Neill, who would find international fame the same year in Steven Spielberg's *Jurassic Park*) was not only an artist, but also an author of many books – including the children's classic *The Magic Pudding*. Several of his books were adapted into film, including *The Age of Consent* in 1969 (the year of Lindsay's death) starring James Mason and a young Helen Mirren in a story that covered many of the same themes as *Sirens*. Working tirelessly in Australia in the early 1900s, Lindsay turned out hundreds of paintings and sketches in oils, watercolours and pencils. Sending more than 40 pieces to the US during the war for safekeeping, they were lost in a train fire. The artist simply responded to the news by stating he'd just have to paint some more. His subject matter was almost always sensual or erotic, and *The Crucified Venus*, the work that acts as the catalyst for the movie story, was indeed a genuine drawing depicting a nude woman being nailed to the cross.

Not a million miles away from the psychodrama farce of *Bitter Moon* in concept, if a world away in execution, the role of Anthony Campion required Hugh to once again play the stammering, shy English gent facing up to an unexpected, and wantonly erotic, alien lifestyle. Ironic really, considering that his time at the Piers Gaveston Society – and their many subsequent reunions – would place the real life Hugh firmly on the side of the liberated artist. The movie was shot on location at Lindsay's home in New South Wales – now the Norman Lindsay Gallery and Museum – where he lived and worked up until his death.

If the increasingly pigeonholed movie roles as blushing, stammering English period prudes bothered him, Hugh didn't have time to show it. He left for Australia having auditioned for a new

HITTING THE BIG TIME

romantic comedy, written by Richard Curtis and directed by Mike Newell, that was already the talk of the British film world. Curtis was a fellow Oxford graduate who had climbed his way up through the Eighties comedy boom thanks to work on *Spitting Image*, *Not The Nine O'Clock News*, *Comic Relief* and his hugely successful sitcom *Blackadder*. His only previous entry into the world of movies had been 1989's forgettable farce *The Tall Guy*, in which Jeff Goldblum played the long-suffering straight man to Rowan Atkinson's vicious comedian. Nevertheless, his latest screenplay had created a stir around the British film industry that slowly grew to a roar. The movie had Mike Newell attached to direct, another acolyte of the Mel Smith/Griff Rhys Jones/Rowan Atkinson comedy trinity, and every British actor wanted to be a part of it. The movie was, of course, *Four Weddings And A Funeral*, a shamelessly romantic tale of a bashful Englishman trying to woo a free-spirited American woman over the course of the titular nuptials and burial.

There was no shortage of actors eager for the lead role of Charles, a quintessentially awkward upper-middle-class chap, and though Mike Newell had found his turn in *Bitter Moon* to be exactly what he wanted, Hugh's commitment to *Sirens* almost cost him the opportunity. Luckily, the tortuous and unexpectedly long-winded efforts to raise the relatively tiny £3.5 million budget for *Four Weddings* meant that – with a little schedule juggling – Hugh would now be able to finish *Sirens* and head back to the UK to begin shooting on Four Weddings. Hugh told the *Observer* that when he first read the script, the character Charles was unlike anybody he had ever met, but when he went to the first rehearsal and saw Richard Curtis, it all became clear – it was he.

And so it came to pass that Hugh ended his Australian adventure and jetted back around the globe to begin production on *Four Weddings and a Funeral* almost immediately. Fully aware of the potential of the movie, and the pressure of being the romantic male lead, Hugh was less than confident as he sat down for the first cast rehearsals.

He later revealed that the first read-through of the script was pretty traumatic – he'd been hoisted out of nowhere to take this role and found himself surrounded by some of Britain's most wonderful actors and producers. He recalls how a woman from the Working Title Production

HUGH GRANT

HITTING THE BIG TIME

Company who was sitting next to him had written in her note book 'Hugh Grant...more Ironic???' Hugh reminds her of it every time they meet.

The budget may have taken a long time to raise, but it was still a tiny amount for even a British motion picture - barely enough to cover the basic costs of making the movie. Shoots were arranged to minimise the number of overnight stays for cast and crew – Hugh went home to his flat at the end of most days filming – and "exotic" locations such as Scotland were faked by a quick jaunt up the M1 to Birmingham.

The movie was completed in a hectic 36 day shoot, and coming right on the back of his work on *Sirens* and the lengthy travelling involved for that project, it was an exhausting experience. As the film went into post-production to be edited and finished off, Hugh took the opportunity to enjoy the London nightlife – often with Liz Hurley, who was having a rather eventful year herself, having signed up for her first movie role opposite Wesley Snipes in the American action thriller *Passenger 57*. It was to be a brief respite, however.

January 1994 saw *Four Weddings* open the prestigious Sundance Film Festival in Utah. The festival, started in 1978 as the US Film Festival,

HITTING THE BIG TIME

had become the lifeblood of independent and international cinema in the United States and each year brought a new influx of hopeful young talents and overseas projects hoping to find a credible route to Hollywood success. In 1985 the festival was taken over by the Sundance Institute, an equally altruistic organisation set up by Robert Redford (and named after his famous character from the 1969 western *Butch Cassidy and the Sundance Kid*).

Opening the festival was considered an honour, if a sometimes dubious one. Many movies wilted under the intense attention – including Mike Newell's previous movie, *Into The West*, which had opened the 1993 festival and then sunk without trace. *Four Weddings* would face no such fate. The movie was a resounding success with the festival audience, and word began to spread about the inexpensive romantic comedy from England. Hugh was in attendance, and was soon inundated with interview requests – which he strived gamely to honour, despite being stricken with flu and exhaustion. Needless to say, the US press – used to dealing with the icily professional interview techniques of Hollywood megastars – were bowled over by the unfailingly polite and mockingly self-deprecating actor. The US distributors were so impressed and excited by the movie's critical reception that they pulled the release forward to March 1994, and embarked on an advertising blitz that centred around the charming "new" British star, Hugh Grant. By the time the movie was ready to open, it seemed as if every newspaper and every magazine in the country had a Hugh Grant interview and the boy from Chiswick was suddenly the most in-demand face in America.

The movie was a smash, raking in $52 million during its American run, and topping $200 million worldwide – a staggering fifty times the original budget. It was an international sensation, bringing the Midas touch to everything connected to it – from the hotels featured in the story, which saw an influx of American tourists, to the poetry of W.H. Auden, memorably read aloud at the movie's emotional funeral by John Hannah, and subsequently repackaged in a volume which raced to the top of the bestsellers list.

A song from the movie, a re-recording of the Trogg's classic *Love Is All Around* by Scottish pop group Wet Wet Wet, rocketed to the top of the chart and remained in the number one slot for 15 weeks. All told, the single sold an astonishing 1.78 million copies securing it a place in the pantheon of biggest selling singles of all time. Reg Presley, lead singer of The Trogg's and writer of *Love Is All Around*, as well as rock classics such as *Wild Thing*, put some of his windfall of royalties from the song's renewed success to interesting use – he invested it in research into the crop circle phenomenon, a mystery that had long intrigued him.

Even Hugh's haircut became a talking point, his limp, floppy fringe becoming an icon in itself – everyone wanted a haircut like Hugh Grant.

Hugh later explained that the hairdresser had in fact created a truly horrible haircut for Hugh's character Charles so that it would be harder for him to win the heart of Andie McDowell.

In the wake of *Four Weddings* runaway success, *Sirens*, filmed first but released second, revamped its poster campaign to play up Hugh's lead role, rather than the naked presence of supermodel Elle MacPherson, which had previously thought to have been the movie's strongest selling point. Though it didn't come close to the level of business that *Four Weddings* was generating, *Sirens* was perfectly placed to ride the wave of

HITTING THE BIG TIME

Hughmania to modest success.

When *Four Weddings* finally opened on 13 May in the UK, ironically billed as America's favourite movie, Hugh and Elizabeth caused yet another wave of publicity at the gala premiere when Liz opted for a daring Versace dress held together by oversized safety pins. The pair insisted it was an uncalculated last-minute wardrobe choice, but the frenzy surrounding "that dress" ensured that Liz got to share the *Four Weddings* limelight as well, and they were swiftly elevated to the ranks of great showbiz couples.

The attention soon became frustrating though, as tabloid adulation inevitably soured into tabloid obsession. Some of it was harmless, if annoying, such as the persistent rumour that Hugh was tipped to star in the forthcoming revival of the Bond franchise, *Goldeneye*. What began as idle speculation in the movie industry was soon passed off as fact by the press, even though Hugh had never been contacted about the role – or even had much interest in it.

He told the BBC that he didn't really think that Bond films were quite his cup of tea. He added, however, that he might feel differently if the films returned to their roots and were set in

HITTING THE BIG TIME

the Fifties and Sixties, when the characters, costumes and attitudes were true to the original Ian Fleming books – which he loved. The role, of course, went to Pierce Brosnan, who had originally been signed to take over from Roger Moore before his TV commitments forced him out of the running. Reports of Hugh's interest in the espionage genre weren't completely inaccurate though, as among many of his new proposed projects, he was attached to the big screen remake of *The Saint* for some time, before Val Kilmer finally took the role.

But there was also a darker side to this newfound fame, and much of it was aimed at Liz Hurley. Now considered fair game by the press, she found her past being thoroughly ransacked for any tales of misbehaviour during her youth as a punk on the not-so-mean streets of Reading. Newspapers offered cash for anyone who had "romped" with the star to come forward and tell their story.

Hugh's character in *Four Weddings and a Funeral* was also blurring with his real life personality – at least as far as the press and public were concerned. Many assumed that the disarmingly nice Charles must be a lot like the real Hugh Grant, an assumption helped along by

HUGH GRANT

HITTING THE BIG TIME

Hugh's modest and accommodating interview style. With a filmography filled with daft toffs and well-meaning chaps, typecasting was already a problem. "Being typecast may be partly my fault", he reminisced, "because I've always chosen jobs more on the basis of, 'is it well written and entertaining rather than is it interesting and stretching for me as an actor?' And that has meant that I probably have repeated myself too often."

With *Four Weddings* still raking in the cash at the box office, the perception of Hugh as a simpering nice upper-class fellow was already ingrained in the mind of audiences and Hugh, the sharp-tongued, football-loving, middle-class son of a carpet salesman, wanted to do something that would dispel the misconception. Luckily, old friends had just such a solution ready to go.

An Awfully Big Adventure was not only another period British romp, it was also directed by Mike Newell and featured a cast of dependable British thesps such as Alan Rickman and Prunella Scales to boot. A scathing satire set amongst bickering amateur actors in 1940s Liverpool, the movie showcased a different side of Hugh to his endearingly clumsy turn as *Four Weddings*' Charles. The story, based on the book by Beryl Bainbridge, followed a

HITTING THE BIG TIME

naïve young girl called Stella who finds solace from an unsatisfying home life by ingratiating herself into the local theatre company, where she falls for the director, Meredith Potter, oblivious to his homosexuality. The story ends on a bleak note, as Stella throws herself at the closest thing the theatre group has to a celebrity, losing her virginity to the callous actor, before taking final, fatal steps to deal with her broken heart.

As the bitterly manipulative Meredith, Hugh drew heavily on his time with the Nottingham Playhouse, making sure to skewer all the precious flaws of the insular and backstabbing provincial theatre scene. Indeed, the character was so vicious and cruel, and such a complete about-face from his public persona, that Hugh had to convince Mike Newell he was the man for the part.

The movie was released in 1995 but, with its peculiar mixture of biting comedy and depressing tragedy, it failed to garner enough mainstream attention to assuage the world's view of Hugh as a professional Mr. Nice Guy.

The post-*Four Weddings* fallout saw Hugh keeping suitably busy, as he tried to capitalise on his newfound celebrity while showcasing as many different sides to his talent as the rigid confines of

HITTING THE BIG TIME

showbiz expectation would allow. This wasn't always easy. "There's a lot of mediocre romantic comedy scripts out there," he would later explain on American television's *The Early Show*. "But if you really want a good, sharp one you've got to wait and you've got to work." Also released in 1995 was *The Englishman Who Went Up A Hill But Came Down A Mountain* which, coming on the heels of *Four Weddings and a Funeral* and *An Awfully Big Adventure*, suggested that Hugh's movies seemed to be competing with each other to see which could get away with the wordiest title. The film saw Hugh reunited with *Sirens* co-star Tara Fitzgerald, and was another "based on actual events" light comedy requiring Hugh to wheel out his "Golly, Crikey" persona once again.

He starred as Reginald Anson, a cartographer who – in 1917 – was sent to a Welsh village to officially measure what the locals claimed to be "the first Welsh mountain". His measurements reveal that the proud mound falls just short of Ordnance Survey mountain criteria, much to the chagrin of the expectant villagers. Unwilling to admit defeat, the colourful townsfolk come up with increasingly farcical schemes to keep him from leaving (which is were the substantial charms of

HITTING THE BIG TIME

Tara Fitzgerald come into play) while they cheat and add the required height to their hill by hand.

As light as a soufflé, the movie performed reasonably well – no doubt boosted by the Hugh factor – but its gentle charms, falling into the narrow genre occupied by similarly provincial British comedies like *Whiskey Galore*, failed to win an international audience outside of the usual Anglophile circles.

Launched under the long shadow of *Four Weddings*, it seemed to the media and the man in the street that this flow of ensuing Hugh projects was littered with disappointment, but the truth was that it was *Four Weddings* which was the aberration – an unrepeatable and fortuitous mixture of the right film at the right time – and the subsequent movies were simply the lingering holdovers from the pre-fame years, suddenly too small for their A-list star. Though most had been filmed and released in the aftermath, many of the deals had already been signed before *Four Weddings* exploded.

With his name and face on the lips of every showbiz columnist and casting agent in Hollywood, it was time to make a concerted effort for that Holy Grail of overseas actors – "breaking

HITTING THE BIG TIME

America". Having moved agents to the LA-based Creative Artists Agency, home to the A-list likes of Steven Spielberg, Tom Cruise and Julia Roberts, megastar success was within tantalising reach. Hugh could now command a salary of around $6 million per movie, and had a "first refusal" deal on developing new scripts with the Castle Rock production company (run by director Rob Reiner and the home of hit comedies like *When Harry Met Sally*). Like many actors eager to take the reins of their career, Hugh had even founded his own production company in London, together with Liz Hurley, called Simian Films. The company name, meaning "ape like", was jokingly based on Hugh's appearance.

Liz Hurley regularly joked to the press that she thought Hugh looked like a chimpanzee – that his small ears are placed very high on his head. A little humiliating, she added, but true.

The first truly post-Four *Weddings* Hugh Grant vehicle was *Nine Months*, his first Hollywood movie and one obviously designed to make the most of his US popularity. It was written and directed by Chris Columbus, the blockbuster director who had given the world the comedy hits *Home Alone* and *Mrs Doubtfire*, and would go on to produce and direct the first two Harry Potter movies. Interestingly, Hugh's two-time collaborator Mike Newell would sign on to direct the fourth in the series, *The Goblet of Fire*, and Hugh himself was long rumoured for the role of grandstanding wizard celebrity Gilderoy Lockhart eventually played by Kenneth Branagh in the second movie, *The Chamber of Secrets*.

Nine Months found Hugh as Samuel Faulkner; a child psychologist who freaks out when he discovers his girlfriend of five years is pregnant. Utterly unprepared for fatherhood, the couple split up, until Samuel has an epiphany and realises that he loves her just in time for the expected sentimental reunion before the credits roll. A remake of the 1994 French hit *Neuf Mois*, if the plot of *Nine Months* was formulaic romantic comedy fare, the cast was rather impressive and a good indicator of just how high Hugh's stock had risen in Hollywood. Julianne Moore, star of Robert Altman's award-winning *Short Cuts* only two years earlier and an actress known more for serious drama than lightweight comedic roles, was on board as Rebecca, Samuel's pregnant lover. Jeff Goldblum was in support as Samuel's friend, an eccentric artist, and comic legend Robin Williams provided a powerhouse cameo as the Russian doctor delivering the baby. Brash American comedian Tom Arnold was also in the cast, and formed an unlikely friendship with Hugh, as both were frequently in the tabloids – Arnold for his tempestuous relationship with TV star Roseanne, and Hugh for his sudden rise to fame and exotic girlfriend. It was lucky they were friends, as while filming a fight scene in the movie, Arnold accidentally punched Hugh in the face.

He described what happened to CNN, saying that he completely missed his target and punched Hugh right on the nose and that's why the scene looked so realistic. As droll and deadpan as ever Hugh added that all actors have their own personal survival tricks and that Tom's was to beat up the nearest English person, which happened to be him.

Hugh may have sat slightly awkwardly in the modern-day American setting, the only Brit in a very American movie and his now-expected bumbling Anglicism heightened even more by the contrast, but the movie was a warm-hearted, star-studded romantic comedy featuring the hottest face in Hollywood primed for the profitable summer season. What could go wrong?

6

Divine intervention

HUGH GRANT

DIVINE INTERVENTION

I n the early hours of 27 June 1995, mere weeks before the opening of *Nine Months*, Hugh was arrested by two police officers on Hollywood's Sunset Boulevard, about a mile from the famous Mann's Chinese Theatre, and its forecourt of celebrity palm prints. He was in town recording the expected press and television interviews to coincide with the planned release of Nine Months on 12 July. But on this fateful night, the plain clothes officers cruising Hollywood's infamous red light district had observed him in a white BMW. When Hugh pulled over, inviting known prostitute Divine Brown (real name:

DIVINE INTERVENTION

Estelle Thompson) to get into the car, then driving to a quiet residential street, the police moved in. For what the officer's observed through the car window, he was charged with "lewd conduct".

By the time the sun rose the next day, the story had made its way from the police press office to every newspaper in the English-speaking world – and beyond. A statement hastily put together by Hugh's publicists read: "Last night I did something completely insane. I have hurt people I love and embarrassed people I work with. For both things I am more sorry than I can say." The fallout was immense. Hugh was released without having to pay bail, and headed away from the spotlights to try and piece things back together. Liz Hurley did the same on the other side of the Atlantic, something made harder by the fact it coincided with her public launch as the new face of Estee Lauder cosmetics. Once the dust had settled somewhat, Hugh flew back to England to be with Liz and tackle the future of their relationship – naturally, the paparazzi were there, lenses poked through bushes and car windows, to try and capture the beleaguered couple. Meanwhile, the press descended on Sunset Boulevard to track down the other party

DIVINE INTERVENTION

involved in the scandal, waving chequebooks in order to secure Divine Brown's side of the story, with the *News of the World* winning the exclusive kiss-and-tell scoop.

Overnight Hugh had gone from being the quintessential Englishman abroad, to just another celebrity mired in sleaze, his fall from grace all the more shocking because of his sensitive image. The UK tabloids went into overdrive while the US talk shows, which Hugh had been diligently appearing on only weeks before, now used him as a figure of fun, a topical joke to start the show. Such scandals were hardly rare in showbiz circles, and in the media circus of the Nineties it had become expected for the celebrity involved to either refuse interviews and wait for the storm in a teacup to disperse (usually when the next famous face was caught out), or to sell their hand-wringing life story to the highest bidder to try and explain their indiscretion away as a momentary lapse brought on by long-buried emotional damage.

Hugh took the opposite approach, and instead made another tour of America's leading entertainment chat shows to openly and honestly apologise for his slip up.

HUGH GRANT

DIVINE INTERVENTION

He talked earnestly about the event, saying that although he could accept some of the explanations that people had offered, such as stress, pressure and loneliness, he knew that these weren't the real reasons for his behaviour. He wanted to come clean and admit that what he did was simply shabby and dishonourable.

When he returned to Jay Leno's light-hearted *The Tonight Show*, forgiving fans waited outside the studio with banners of support. On the show, of which Hugh was – and is – a popular and regular guest, Hugh elaborated more on his regret. "I think you know in life what's a good thing to do and what's a bad thing. I did a bad thing and there you have it," he confided. When pressed on the tabloid stories about Liz Hurley's assumed rage, Hugh continued, "She's been amazing about it. Contrary to what I read in the paper today, she's been very supportive and we're going to try to work it out."

At a time when it was fashionable to pass the blame for mistakes onto an unhappy childhood or other external forces, Hugh's refreshing candour – delivered with customary twinkling charm – was enough to turn the tide of public opinion. His image might not have been polished to its previous

DIVINE INTERVENTION

sheen, but it was considerably less tarnished than it had been on the morning of 27 June.

Nine Months opened under a glare of scrutiny, as pundits waited to see if Hugh's newfound notoriety would impact on box office receipts. The reviews were largely negative, not because of infamy, but because the film just didn't work as a comedy. Many reviewers pointed to the uneven tone – veering between broad slapstick and mawkish sentiment – as well as the formulaic plot, which failed to bring any charm to the predictable yarn. Almost all the reviews agreed on one thing though – none of this was the fault of the cast, who were largely credited for doing their best with an uninspiring script.

Roger Ebert, one of America's most famous critics even exonerated the cast saying that it was unfair to expect the cast to make something out of nothing.

Nine Months brought in just under $70 million at US cinemas, not enough to qualify it as a blockbuster, but enough to confirm that Hugh's appeal had weathered the media storm.

Hugh Grant as Daniel Cleaver with Renée Zellwegger as Bridget Jones in a scene from the highly-successful film, 'Bridget Jones's Dairy' (2001). Grant wowed audiences as Bridget's boss.

Hugh Grant is one of the most successful British actors, appearing in numerous films including: 'Sense and Sensibility', 'Notting Hill', 'About a Boy' and 'Love Actually'.

Liz Hurley in 'that' dress – a daring Versace gown.
The couple were attending the gala premiere for
'Four Weddings and a Funeral' (1994)

Hugh Grant as the Prime Minister with his love-interest played by Martine McCutcheon, in the successful hit of 2003 'Love Actually'.

7

Reputation restored

HUGH GRANT

REPUTATION RESTORED

The months rolled on, and what had been hot gossip slowly became old news. As this tumultuous year came to a close, Hugh had much more pleasant reasons to be back in the press – two more movies, both representing a return to comfortingly familiar territory.

Restoration was a movie of several reunions, and although Hugh took only a small part in the period romp set in the court of Charles II, it allowed him to work once again with his *Sirens* co-star Sam Neill, playing King Charles, and – for the first time since those now-distant Oxford days – reunite with his first ever director, the enthusiastic student

REPUTATION RESTORED

filmmaker Mike Hoffman, who had recognised Hugh's potential way back in 1982 for *Privileged*. Hoffman had not grown into a prolific filmmaker, but he had the Golden Globe nominated Sally Field and Kevin Kline comedy *Soapdish* to his credit, and would go on to direct George Clooney in *One Fine Day*, and a star-studded movie adaptation of Shakespeare's *A Midsummer Night's Dream*.

Restoration, based on the Booker Prize nominated novel by Rose Tremain, told the tale of Robert Merivel, a 17th century doctor who finds favour in the King's court and is eventually obliged to marry the monarch's mistress in order to provide cover for their adultery. Falling in love with his bride of convenience, the doctor is cast out of the favourable society and rediscovers his passion for medicine among the poor of plague-era London. The witty title referred to both the Restoration period in which the story takes place, and also the restoration of Merivel's true calling in life after succumbing to temptation. With Sam Neill as the King, the troubled US actor Robert Downey Jr took the lead role of Merivel, with Hugh content to provide support as the shifty courtier Elias Finn along with venerable British acting stalwarts such as Ian McKellen as

REPUTATION RESTORED

Merivel's servant and Ian McDiarmid (best known as the villainous Emperor in the *Star Wars* trilogy).

The movie was well-liked by critics, who admired Hoffman's sense of grandeur on a relatively small budget, including such daring set-pieces as the Great Fire of London, and the rather subtle AIDS metaphor running through Merivel's willingness to rediscover his healing ways against the ominous backdrop of the Black Death. While the majority of the praise was directed towards Downey Jr and the other leads, that may have been precisely what Hugh wanted – a chance to repay Hoffman for his foresight, and to ease himself back into acting without drawing too much attention.

Early 1996 brought another familiar project – a period drama, drawn from classic English literature. This time it was to the works of Jane Austen that Hugh found himself drawn, and her 1811 novel *Sense and Sensibility*, published just six years before her death at the age of 42 and now brought to the screen from a script adapted by Emma Thompson (written many years before, as a labour of love), and directed by the acclaimed Taiwanese director Ang Lee, his first English-language movie after the Oscar-nominated *Eat, Drink, Man, Woman.*

The story, a classic tale of three very different sisters forced to face up to matters of love and marriage through a change in fortune, offered plenty of room for an impressive ensemble cast and once again Hugh was able to slot into a reassuring environment without the burden of being the 'big name star'. Thompson had actually written the role of Edward Ferrar with Hugh in mind, marking their third movie together following *Impromptu* and *The Remains of the Day*. Talking to Mirabella Magazine, Thompson described Hugh as "repellently gorgeous" and when asked why he'd been chosen, simply replied, "He's much prettier than I am." Indeed, The Jane Austen Society told Thompson that they thought Hugh was too handsome and charming for the part of the famously dull Edward!

Thompson also took the nominal lead role as Elinor Dashwood, second eldest of the sisters, with a young Kate Winslet, in only her second movie role after her turn in 1994's *Heavenly Creatures* from *Lord of the Rings* director Peter Jackson, as the youngest sister, Marianne. As the rather dull Edward Ferrar, one of the least remarkable

REPUTATION RESTORED

romantic heroes in English literature, Hugh was able to let the ladies take the limelight in the typically female-centred Austen story, sharing the supporting responsibility with his *Awfully Big Adventure* co-star Alan Rickman.

As veterans of the movie business, and considerable authorities on the source material, both Emma Thompson and Hugh would make suggestions to director Ang Lee for certain scenes or shots, something that came as a shock to the Asian filmmaker.

He later explained that as a director in Taiwan he would be expected to make all the decisions, but here everyone gets involved and no one questions it. He added that *Sense And Sensibility* was the first time he had had to convince people to do what he wanted. Despite the initial communication problems, the shoot was a happy, friendly and harmonious one – even though it coincided with Thompson's well-publicised divorce from fellow actor and director Kenneth Branagh.

Sense and Sensibility proved to be a huge hit, making over £75 million on a budget of less than £10 million. It was nominated for seven Oscars – with Emma Thompson winning the Best Adapted

REPUTATION RESTORED

Screenplay award – as well as BAFTAs for Best Film, Best Actress for Emma Thompson, and Best Supporting Actress for Kate Winslet, and Golden Globes for Best Motion Picture Drama and Best Screenplay.

Once again, Hugh took a back seat, with the accolades laid at the feet of Emma Thompson and Ang Lee for their marvellous adaptation and vision, but the deserved success of the movie had reaffirmed Hugh as an actor of class and integrity – not just a movie star – and he was now ready to attack his career with renewed vigour and a new sense of purpose.

It was time to take control.

8

A star is reborn

HUGH GRANT

A STAR IS REBORN

With his brush with scandal now behind him, Hugh was ready to start using his star power to make the films he wanted to make. Hugh and Liz's production company, Simian Films, had been understandably quiet since its formation in 1994, but with both now determined to look to the future, it was the ideal time to put the company into action. And so the first Simian Films project to roll into production was a script that Liz had picked up previously. Based on the novel by Michael Palmer, and adapted by Tony Gilroy (who would later write the spy thriller *The Bourne Identity* for Matt Damon), *Extreme Measures*

A STAR IS REBORN

represented a complete change of pace for Hugh. A modern-day medical conspiracy thriller along the lines of the 1978 Michael Douglas movie *Coma*, it would require Hugh to abandon his highly marketable upper-class image for something more traditionally heroic.

As Dr Guy Lathan, a British doctor working in a New York hospital, Hugh starred as an idealistic and moral emergency room surgeon who uncovers a grisly conspiracy when the body of a man who died in his ER vanishes without trace. Digging into the mystery, he discovers a horrific trade in homeless people, and gruesome illegal medical experiments to boot, all overseen by the hospitals most respected surgeon, Dr Myrick. Needless to say, as with any good movie conspiracy, the shadowy figures behind the skulduggery don't take kindly to the meddling and the good doctor is forced to fight for his life – and the truth.

On paper, it's certainly not a role that immediately called to mind everyone's favourite bumbling romantic, requiring Hugh to all but abandon this popular image and become something of an action hero. He and Liz spent over a year developing the script, fine tuning the character, to the point where it was something

HUGH GRANT

A STAR IS REBORN

Hugh could do – and have audiences believe in him.

As both a producer and star, *Extreme Measures* required Hugh to juggle his performance with the day-to-day logistics of getting the movie made and managing the $38 million budget. As well as being responsible for casting decisions and ensuring everything ran smoothly, Hugh and Liz shouldered the creative burden of getting the film made their way – and liked it! "I've been frustrated for years by just being wheeled on as an actor," Hugh explained. "It's really nice to be able to legitimately have my say in all the other departments and have control over how the thing comes out. That little taste of power was very delicious."

As director they hired Michael Apted, a fellow Brit with a distinguished career straddling intelligent drama and rousing adventure. His previous hits had included the Oscar-winning *Gorillas In The Mist*, the thriller *Gorky Park* and the Jodie Foster movie, *Nell*. He would, of course, go on to helm the 1999 James Bond adventure *The World Is Not Enough*.

Casting the movie was an exciting experience for both Hugh and Liz. In the roles of the corrupt cop and crooked FBI agent who help the hospital keep a lid on their missing cadavers, they chose a

A STAR IS REBORN

pair of well respected character actors, known for their commanding presence, Bill Nunn and David Morse. Nunn was a familiar face from many of Spike Lee's movies – including *Mo' Better Blues* and *Do The Right Thing*. Morse had just co-starred in the Sean Connery action movie *The Rock* as well as the mind-bending Bruce Willis sci-fi drama *Twelve Monkeys*. Together they gave the movie's muscle a level of intelligence that lifted the action elements to a more believable level. The names given to these two characters – Detective Burke and Agent Hare – was an obvious and deliberate nod to the historical grave robbers Burke and Hare, who stole freshly bodies and sold them to the medical establishment in 19th century Edinburgh – stooping to cold-blooded murder when supplies ran low. As another little nod to the more eagle-eyed viewer, Canadian director David Cronenberg – famous for his arthouse horror movies – appeared in a cameo as the head of a medical tribunal.

For the pivotal role of the morally slippery Nobel Prize winning Dr Myrick, they wanted someone who could bring out the ambiguity in the character. The doctor wasn't an out-and-out villain, and though his methods had led him down the dark alley of criminality, his motives were not purely evil. Indeed, his aim – much like those who purchased the dead from the real life Burke and Hare – was to further the reaches of medicine, regardless of the ethical cost. During the long development of the script, both Hugh and Liz knew that screen legend Gene Hackman would be ideal for the part, but didn't dare presume he'd grace their little thriller with his heavyweight presence. To their surprise, he did, something that thrilled Hugh the producer, but terrified Hugh the actor. "We were jubilant when he took the part," he admitted to Eclectica Magazine, "but from then on I was gibbering at the prospect of having to play against this guy."

The movie would also be the closest that Hugh had come to being an action hero, not including his clumsy sword battle with a snake woman in *Lair of the White Worm*, as his *Extreme Measures* character was required to race through the streets on a motorbike. The reality was rather less than inspiring for Hugh. "You sit in your trailer all day while your double does it and then you go outside to shout 'NO!' and you go back to your trailer," he told Combustible Celluloid. "It's crap. It's not that I'm precious about acting, but you like to be at least semi-occupied during the day."

HUGH GRANT

A STAR IS REBORN

The movie opened in September 1996 in America to a damp reception - "silly and far-fetched" scoffed *Rolling Stone* magazine, though they had to admit that Hugh "looks good with a stethoscope and plays with quiet strength". The movie failed to make back even half it's budget during its US theatrical run, with audiences apparently unwilling to pay to see Hugh as a crusading hero – despite his performance receiving largely positive notices, the *New York Times* noting that Hugh was "able to hurtle through this intrigue without altogether losing his sardonic edge".

The relative failure of *Extreme Measures* – and the insistence by the press to continue referencing his dalliance with Divine Brown – may have caused Hugh to reflect on the directions his career was taking. He had been working non-stop for more than ten years, often stretching himself across three or four films a year, as well as their attendant international publicity tours. For someone who often told interviewers that acting had been an accidental career choice, it was time to take stock and become more selective with the projects he undertook. So it was that in 1997 Hugh took a deliberate step back from the treadmill and concentrated on finding movies that would allow

A STAR IS REBORN

him to leave the Posh Hugh persona behind for good. In the fast-moving world of movie stardom, this was a bold move. Many stars have stepped out of the limelight, only to find it impossible to re-enter its balmy glow afterwards. In particular, Hugh headed to the Simian Films office to continue development on a mafia comedy that he was keen to star in.

For over two years, Hugh was absent from cinema and TV screens, though he remained in the public eye somewhat thanks to his involvement in the headline generating machine that was his private life. Liz's role in the Mike Myers comedy *Austin Powers: International Man of Mystery*, clad in a sexy tight leather jumpsuit for much of the spy spoofs running time, ensured that Hugh's name was still in people's minds even if it was his girlfriend who was receiving all the attention.

9

Business and the blue-eyed boy

HUGH GRANT

BUSINESS AND THE BLUE-EYED BOY

It took another Richard Curtis comedy – a love letter to his own beloved London borough, Notting Hill – to tempt Hugh out of his self-imposed exile in 1999, the shift in location from the fairy tale country manors of *Four Weddings and a Funeral* to a more bohemian city setting possibly fitting in better with Hugh's preferred perception of himself. The story also probably appealed to Hugh's self-deprecating and barbed sense of humour. He starred as William Thacker, an unassuming proprietor of a small travel bookshop in the titular Notting Hill. A chance meeting with Anna Scott, the world's

BUSINESS AND THE BLUE-EYED BOY

favourite Hollywood actress, leads to a surprising romance and forces William's utterly ordinary life to accommodate the glare of publicity attached to dating a celebrity.

You didn't have to dig too deeply to see the irony in this role – and it gave Hugh the perfect chance to exorcise his media demons, turning his torments at the hands of the tabloids into fuel for a comic performance. In a perfect piece of casting, his romantic lead – the most famous actress in the world – was played by Julia Roberts, the most famous actress in the world. Also along for the ride was up and coming Welsh actor Rhys Ifans as William's grungily exuberant flatmate, with a sprinkling of famous faces – Alec Baldwin, Matthew Modine, and Simon Callow (the "Funeral" in *Four Weddings and a Funeral*) – taking advantage of the movie's 'movie within a movie' conceit to send themselves up in cameo roles.

The movie was filmed on the actual streets of Notting Hill. William's house – with its famous blue door – was actually Richard Curtis' house, while William's bookshop was, in reality, a butcher shop two doors away from Richard Curtis' production office. The blue door became such a famous part of the movie that it was later auctioned for Christies.

HUGH GRANT

BUSINESS AND THE BLUE-EYED BOY

Despite the shift in location from the more genteel Four Weddings, the movie wasn't too far removed from the winning formula – something Richard Curtis himself admitted during a BAFTA writing workshop in 2002. "I'm disappointed in myself," he joked. "You can't imagine the shock when I realised *Notting Hill* was exactly the same as *Four Weddings and a Funeral*; it's Hugh Grant, there are five friends, it's got an American girl who comes in and out of the movie..."

Formulaic it may have been, but *Notting Hill* was obviously just what audiences had been waiting for. Opening in the summer of 1999 against box office behemoths like *Star Wars Episode I* and the sequel to Austin Powers (in which Liz briefly reprised her role as Vanessa Kensington – before revealing herself to be a 'fembot' and exploding) *Notting Hill* provided a mature and romantic alternative to space battles and sexual innuendo, and stood its ground with great success. Costing $42 million to make (a not inconsiderable tenfold increase from *Four Weddings*) the sweetly romantic tale made more than half that amount in its first weekend in the US alone. It soon overtook *Four Weddings* as the most successful British movie of all time (though

121

many pundits noted that the funding actually came from America) bringing in a staggering $247 million worldwide.

Hugh had returned from his time out with the biggest hit of his career, and was refreshed and ready to dive into the mafia project he'd been developing.

Mickey Blue Eyes began life as a comedy about a Jewish-American lawyer who marries into a mafia family. Like most screenplays, it floated around Hollywood for a while, trying to find a home. When the script landed on the desk of Simian Films, Hugh and Liz recognised the potential and began reworking the central premise from American lawyer to English art dealer, reasoning that the contrast between uptight Englishman and New York gangsters would be funnier and fresher. Hugh was fully aware that the idea of him in a mafia movie was just ridiculous enough to work. "I find it hard to understand why Scorsese has never called," he joked to the SplicedWire online news service. "You know, given the natural menace I bring to the screen."

Hugh was to star as Michael Felgate, another Englishman in New York, this time working for a major auction house. When he proposes to Gina,

BUSINESS AND THE BLUE-EYED BOY

his teacher girlfriend, he discovers that her father is Frank Vitale, a major player in the mob. Welcomed into "The Family" in more ways than one, Michael finds himself obliged to help sell off the gruesomely awful paintings by the son of the local Godfather, helping to launder money for the mafia at the same time – contrary to the express wishes of Gina, who is ashamed of her father's connections. Reluctantly dragged into the world of organised crime, Frank comes up with a way for his prospective son-in-law to better fit in – as the gangster Mickey Blue Eyes – and begins grooming the fussy Brit for mob notoriety. With the FBI closing in, and gang war on the verge of breaking out in the auction room, it's up to Michael to try and keep his fiancée, his father-in-law, gangsters and cops away from each other.

Having gone through the Simian Films anglicising program, Mickey Blue Eyes emerged as a combination of classic British drawing room farce, complete with dropped-trouser misunderstandings, and American gangster movies, complete with shootings and midnight body disposal. It was impeccable timing as well – this was the year of the Mafia revival, with acclaimed TV show *The Sopranos* debuting on the HBO channel, while Robert De Niro

BUSINESS AND THE BLUE-EYED BOY

and Billy Crystal teamed up for the "gangster in therapy" comedy *Analyze This*. Laughing at the mob was the thing to do in '99, it seemed.

For the part of avuncular mobster Frank Vitale, Hugh and Liz literally stumbled into the man for the job. While eating lunch in Hollywood and discussing the project, they bumped into James Caan, and realised immediately that he was their Frank. Caan had rocketed to fame as the quick-tempered Sonny Corleone in Francis Ford Coppola's operatic 1972 gangster epic *The Godfather*, and his violent, bullet-riddled demise in that movie is still seared into the memory of movie fans to this day. Born and bred in The Bronx, Caan was actually the product of Jewish and Irish parents but his role as the doomed Corleone was so convincing that he was twice awarded the title "Italian-American of the Year". "I grew up with everybody Italian in my my neighbourhood," Caan explained to the Calgary Sun. "If you talk with a Brooklyn accent, people automatically think you're Italian." Never afraid to poke some fun at his "made man" image, Caan liked the script and signed up for the role, with *Basic Instinct* star Jeanne Tripplehorne joining the cast as his daughter and Hugh's on-screen

BUSINESS AND THE BLUE-EYED BOY

fiancée. The rest of the cast was easily filled out with a roster of Hollywood's favourite tough guy gangster actors – many of them moonlighting on *The Sopranos* at the same time – and James Fox as Hugh's ditzy boss.

Meanwhile, Hugh and Liz were having trouble finding a director that they believed could capture both the English and American humour required to make the concept work. "I talked to all the top comedy directors in Hollywood", Hugh said of their long search, "and I hated them all. I thought they all wanted to make it schmaltzy." In the end, the solution came to them via a mutual friend – Mike Myers. The comedian recommended Kelly Makin, a fellow Canadian, and director of the cult comedy troupe *The Kids in the Hall*. Makin had directed the group's self-titled TV series as well as their offbeat big screen debut *Brain Candy*, and shared the uniquely transatlantic sense of humour that Myers had also developed – drawn from Canada's exposure to the best of both US and UK television comedy.

Once again, Hugh found himself straddling the creative world of acting and the hard-nosed business requirements of producing. He and Liz were so caught up in making sure they got all the

BUSINESS AND THE BLUE-EYED BOY

Mafioso details correct (including going to dinner with real life Godfathers – "Elizabeth likes to compare jewellery and manicures and stuff" Hugh would joke to reporters) that he left no time for researching his role as an auctioneer. In the end, he sat in on one Sotheby's auction, realised that the superfast chatter of a real auction would be useless on film, and proceeded to do it his own way. This constant racing around, worrying about details, led James Caan to give Hugh the nickname 'Whippy', because he was supposedly always shaking like a whippet. "He was a lot of fun," Caan said in an interview. "He's also very nervous and neurotic. He's very British and I'm very New York. We're kind of oil and water, so we had a good time working together." *Mickey Blue Eyes* opened only two months after *Notting Hill*, and suffered under the shadow of that more marketable blockbuster. The movie wasn't a flop by any means, earning back its $40 million budget over its UK and US release, but nor did it generate much excitement or interest. Reviewers complained that the movie relied too heavily on well-worn stereotypes – the folksy camaraderie of the gangsters, the useless dithering of the English – and the predictable plot covered ground already

BUSINESS AND THE BLUE-EYED BOY

ploughed by the Marlon Brando and Matthew Broderick gangster comedy *The Freshman*. Interestingly, one criticism wasn't that Hugh had strayed too far from his core appeal, but that he didn't go far enough in his seduction by the mob. "If this had been a far darker comedy in which Grant's character finds within himself a capacity for viciousness and violence", wrote Philip Kemp in *Sight & Sound*, "that could have been a Hugh Grant performance worth watching."

The potential for Hugh to meld his affable charm with a more villainous streak – as hinted at in *An Awfully Big Adventure* – would turn out to be a remarkably astute piece of foresight.

1999 also saw Hugh undertaking some delightfully silly TV work, further evidence that his break from the spotlight had renewed his passion for combining work and fun. He joined an all-star voice cast for the US version of the *Comic Relief* festive animation *Hooves of Fire*, from Richard Goleszowski, the Aardman Animation director who had worked on *Wallace and Gromit*, and *Creature Comforts*. Hugh added his vocal talents as the sneeringly superior Blitzen in this modern twist on the tale of Rudolph the Red-Nosed Reindeer (now renamed Robbie). The British version had drawn

BUSINESS AND THE BLUE-EYED BOY

from a rich well of TV comedians, with Alan Partridge creator Steve Coogan taking the Blitzen role. For the US broadcast, Hugh was part of a line-up that featured Britney Spears, Ben Stiller and James Woods.

Also for *Comic Relief*, the comedy charity supported by *Four Weddings* and *Notting Hill*, writer Richard Curtis was *Doctor Who and the Curse of Fatal Death*, an affectionate spoof of the beloved BBC sci-fi series broadcast in four parts throughout 1999's *Comic Relief* telethon. With Rowan Atkinson as Doctor Who, and *Absolutely Fabulous* star Julia Sawalha as his assistant, the 30-minute skit pitted the timelord against the Daleks – and his arch-enemy, The Master. The sketch had great fun with the Doctor's regular face-changing rebirths, introduced in the Sixties to allow the role to be passed on to new actors, and the show's habit of reuniting previous generations of Doctor Who's for special storylines. Hugh cameoed in this light-hearted romp as The Handsome 12th Doctor, alongside Richard E. Grant as The Quite Handsome 10th Doctor, Jim Broadbent as The Shy 11th Doctor and Joanna Lumley as The Female 13th Doctor. Jonathan Pryce hammed it up magnificently as The Master (the seventeenth Master, to be precise). The appearance, inevitably, led to press speculation that Hugh was being groomed for the role in the long-rumoured revival of the show, his presence making it easier to sell overseas. As always, the rumour was nothing more than idle speculation – when the BBC finally brought Doctor Who back, it would be Christopher Eccleston who was announced as the latest owner of the TARDIS.

The 21st century rolled around with a new emphasis on quality over quantity for Hugh. Whereas previous years had seen him appear in three or four movies, from 2000 onwards it would be rare for even two Hugh movies to open in the same year. The first fruits of this shift in focus would be another of Hugh's collaborations with a highly respected director. May saw the US opening of the new Woody Allen movie, *Small Time Crooks*, in which Hugh joined a typical Allen ensemble cast for a return to the style of the director's early screwball comedies. In the movie, a loser crook called Ray Winkler plots to set up a cookie shop as the cover for digging through the wall into the bank next door. The break-in runs into an endless stream of problems, but the cookie business – run by his wife – becomes a booming success and the

BUSINESS AND THE BLUE-EYED BOY

gang finds themselves rich without having to pull off their job. How they cope with their shift in fortunes is the foundation of Allen's most openly comedic movie in many years.

Woody Allen himself was back in front of the camera, as well as behind it, in the role of hapless Ray, with Tracy Ullman playing Frenchie, his cookie-making wife. Hugh sank his teeth into the role of David Grant, an insidious art dealer who moves in on Frenchie when she tries to parlay their newfound wealth into a life among the upper-class. The chance to subvert his charming image, while working with one of his favourite directors, was too good to pass up though Allen's way of approaching Hugh for the role was rather unorthodox.

Hugh recalled that woody Allen didn't telephone him. Instead he sent a fax saying that he was doing a film and that one of the characters was an apparently charming, well bred Englishman who turns out to be a really nasty piece of work and he thought of me.

The movie turned out to be the most successful Woody Allen movie in a decade, and received warmly appreciative reviews from a critical community then wringing their hands over the rise of gross teen comedies like *American Pie*.

HUGH GRANT

BUSINESS AND THE BLUE-EYED BOY

Ironically, having joked about waiting for Martin Scorsese to call while making *Mickey Blue Eyes*, rumours abounded at this time that the legendary director might actually be calling Hugh up for his next movie. Among his many pet projects, Scorsese had always wanted to make a biopic of Dean Martin, the 60s crooner and member of Frank Sinatra's Rat Pack. Covering the singers life from his childhood (as Dino Crocetti) through to his singing career, acting in movies with Jerry Lewis, and his friendship with Sinatra and President Kennedy. The ambitious project got as far as a script, written by Scorsese's frequent collaborator Nic Pileggi, who had also written *Goodfellas* and *Casino* for the director. Tom Hanks was widely considered to be Scorsese's preferred choice for the role of Dean Martin, with John Travolta as Sinatra and Jim Carrey aptly cast as the rubber-faced Jerry Lewis. Hugh was hotly tipped for the part of Peter Lawford, the sole British member of the Rat Pack who married into the Kennedy family earning himself the nickname "Brother-in-Lawford". However, the sheer cost of assembling this group of actors – not to mention fitting a mammoth shoot into their overlapping schedules – meant that the movie never got

BUSINESS AND THE BLUE-EYED BOY

beyond the development stage.

However, this period of artistic triumph was overshadowed by a more painful personal development. On 24 May, only five days after the US opening of *Small Time Crooks*, Hugh and Liz released a statement to the press via Simian Films announcing that they were separating after 13 years together. "It is a mutual and amicable decision", the statement read: "They are to continue to run Simian Films together and they would like to stress that there are no third parties involved". Although the split was described as "temporary", the couple remain friends – though nothing more, and Simian Films have not produced another movie.

The press had a predictable field day, speculating wildly whenever either Hugh or Liz were seen out in public. There was little time for reflection however. Even as the interviews for *Small Time Crooks* wound down, Hugh was preparing to start work on his third movie with Richard Curtis, the movie adaptation of the much-loved novel, *Bridget Jones's Diary*.

Bridget began life as a newspaper column in *The Independent*, written by author Helen Fielding as a first-person confessional from an

BUSINESS AND THE BLUE-EYED BOY

everywoman for the Nineties, obsessively noting down every cigarette smoked, every calorie consumed and every pound lost or gained. From her job on the fringes of London's media industry, to her self-conscious search for Mr. Right, the character struck a chord with a new generation of twenty-something women, and the catchy Bridget-speak soon caught on, with it's withering descriptions of Smug Marrieds and hapless Singletons. Collected as a novel in 1994, *Bridget Jones* was soon a national – and then international – sensation and a movie version was inevitable

Helen Fielding adapted the book herself, handing the screenplay over to Richard Curtis for a polish. Sharon Maguire, a friend of Fielding's who had worked on commercials and documentaries was in the directors chair, and all that was required was the small matter of the cast.

Hugh had resisted signing on as the dashing cad Daniel Cleaver, Bridget's boss, feeling that the script was lacking something.

He wasn't sure that the script was right and for a long time he voiced his concerns that it wasn't working. He urged the producers to bring Richard Curtis on board to help tinker with the script and as soon as he was hired Hugh signed up.

BUSINESS AND THE BLUE-EYED BOY

Once Hugh was satisfied that the film would be up to the standard set by *Four Weddings* and *Notting Hill,* he came onboard. For one thing, it was another chance to play a scoundrel and a rogue, a character the audience didn't want to get the girl for a change.

Cast as the other man vying for Bridget's attention was Colin Firth as the predictable nice guy that Hugh might have played had the movie been made five years earlier. The casting of Firth was a cheeky in-joke as the novel makes constant reference to Bridget's lust for the actor when he played the aloof Mr. D'arcy in the TV adaptation of *Pride and Prejudice.* As the plot of *Bridget Jones's Diary* loosely resembled *Pride and Prejudice,* and Firth's character was again called Darcy (first name Mark this time), the overlap between reality, fiction and movie was in danger of becoming awfully confusing.

Helen Fielding was overjoyed at the casting of the two male leads. "I must admit to jealously violent thoughts towards Bridget since the announcement that she will be canoodling with both of them," she told *The Telegraph.*

Meanwhile, finding the movie Bridget had become a media circus, not unlike the crazy

BUSINESS AND THE BLUE-EYED BOY

guessing games that had pulled Hugh into gossip about the new James Bond in 1995. It was assumed that the role would go to someone like Kate Winslet. In other words, a British actress. "We all had a clear idea of what we were looking for," producer Jonathan Cavendish told *Time Out* magazine, "When Renée walked through the door, we were half thrilled and half appaled; we'd found Bridget, but she was a Texan!"

When it was announced that the meatiest British female role in decades had gone to Renee Zellweger, a Texan, there was uproar from the media. Along with the rest of the cast, Hugh went out of his way to put out the fires.

He stated that at first he, like many others, raised an eyebrow at the proposition. He told how Renee got the accent sorted pretty quickly and after a brief period adopting a Princess Margaret-type voice, she soon got it absolutely right.

Renee not only worked with a dialogue coach (the same one that taught Gwyneth Paltrow for *Sliding Doors*) to transform her accent into a spotless English for the role, she went on a doughnuts and Guinness diet to put on more than 20lbs to convincingly portray the chubby heroine and her battles with the bulge.

HUGH GRANT

BUSINESS AND THE BLUE-EYED BOY

In 2001, the movie opened on the same April day in both Britain and America – Friday 13th. For once, the day brought nothing but good luck, as the movie provided a hat trick for writer Richard Curtis and Hugh. Once again topping $200 million worldwide, the movie was up there with *Four Wedding*s and *Notting Hill* as an example of the best of British movie comedy.

The year also brought sadness for Hugh. In July his mother, Fynvola, lost her battle with cancer and died at the age of 63. "My mother was the most important woman in the world to me and I'm finding it hard to live without her," he said in a statement. He announced that he would be taking another break from acting, to concentrate on writing film scripts and a novel. He admitted that if the scripts never left his desk at least the writing would give him some time to get himself together. He continued that he was looking for something that made him happy and if he found it he may never return to films.

10

Hair today...

HUGH GRANT

HAIR TODAY...

Hugh was now at a point where he could afford to be choosy as to the roles he took. With *Bridget Jones's Diary*, Hugh had finally shown the world that there was more to him than bumbling toffs and literary suitors, and that he could be just as popular playing a selfish swine as he could as a nice guy. For his next movie, Hugh stayed with the world of modern English literature, this time with an adaptation of the Nick Hornby novel, *About A Boy*. Just as *Bridget Jones* had represented the new wave of popular British books for women (or 'chick lit' as the media dubbed it), so Hornby was at the

HAIR TODAY...

forefront of wryly comic observational writing for men. Two of his previous books had already been adapted to the big screen with some success. *High Fidelity*, the tale of one man rummaging through the scraps of his love life for meaning while obsessing over music, had been transplanted to Chicago and starred John Cusack and Catherine Zeta-Jones. *Fever Pitch*, a similarly witty "romance for boys", but with an Arsenal fixated teacher as its confused hero, had starred none other than Colin Firth in 1997.

About A Boy had been hailed as Hornby's most mature book to date, a touching yet honest look at Will, a man who has completely isolated himself from life, living in a state of extended adolescence and shallow indulgence on the back of royalties from a novelty Christmas hit recorded by his father. Deciding that a single parent support group would be an ideal place to pick up vulnerable women, he invents a fictional son and begins attending the group sessions. His deceit brings him into contact with Marcus, a wise beyond his years twelve-year-old, and his suicidal hippie mum, Fiona. Slowly but surely, Marcus worms his way into Will's life, and the irresponsible adult learns important lessons about growing up from a child.

HAIR TODAY...

Robert De Niro had snapped up the rights to the novel through his company Tribeca Productions and, following the usual period of pre-production musical chairs, the directing job was finally handed to American brothers Chris and Paul Weitz. The choice of the brothers came as a surprise to many, as up until that point they'd been more famous for the *American Pie* comedies. As it turned out, they had been searching for a 'Billy Wilder' comedy – something cynical, but with an emotional heart – and upon reading the novel, were sure that *About A Boy* was precisely what they were after. Originally the plan was to set the film in London, but bring in a Hollywood-based star, with A-list megastars such as George Clooney and Russell Crowe being bandied around. "Although it was going to be in England, they wanted an American to play that part," Hugh explained when he was interviewed on Inside The Actors Studio. "It never really happened. It never really gelled. So then I sort of tentatively put my hand up and said, 'Well, you know, it might be good, seeing as it is written as an English person, if an English person played it.'"

The part of the hopelessly shallow Will was perfect for Hugh's newfound enthusiasm for characters who weren't immediately likable, and he even found himself relating to Will's lifestyle. "The idea of a man who does nothing has always intrigued me", he explained, "because I spent so many years of my life – especially pre-*Four Weddings* – with a pretty slack life. I can remember being so unemployed that I'd sort of save up going to the chemist as my treat for the afternoon."

Hugh also took advantage of the opportunity to cast off the last remaining vestige of the Posh Hugh image still lingering from *Four Weddings*. For the part of trendy, urban Will the floppy locks and flyaway fringe, which had been his trademark since Oxford, got the chop. "I've always wanted to have short hair," he said when asked about his spiky crop. "Long hair's a pain in the arse, but I never really had the right short haircut. Whenever I tried it I looked like a lesbian."

About A Boy hit cinemas in May 2002 and while not a runaway blockbuster in the vein of *Notting Hill*, it earned solid reviews with much praise being heaped on Hugh's long-awaited shedding of his foppish image. "Watching him work an under-written punch-line around his face – eyes darting, nose twitching – is to watch a master craftsman employing, and enjoying, all the

HAIR TODAY...

tools at his disposal" raved *Empire* magazine.

About A Boy made just under $90 million around the world – quite an achievement for a fairly low-key comedy based on a cult British novel. The movie was even successful enough for the studio to try and turn it into a spin-off sitcom for US television, although the shift to a US cast didn't help it stand out in the cutthroat world of American TV and the show vanished with little fanfare.

His next movie, *Two Weeks Notice*, acts as a handy lesson in just how hard it can be to get a movie off the ground in Hollywood. Hugh had been friends with Sandra Bullock, the star of *Speed* and *While You Were Sleeping*, for some time having crossed paths during a "relationship meeting", a sort of blind date for actors where seemingly compatible stars are introduced to each other in the hopes that a fruitful collaboration will spring forth from the fertile soil of their shared interests. He recalled how he told Sandra Bullock a dirty story which must have really disgusted her as he didn't hear from her for three years.

In reality, Sandra (or 'Sandy Bollocks' as Hugh nicknamed her) shared Hugh's love of lowbrow humour – "You just say poop and he starts to giggle," she explained – as well as his

HAIR TODAY...

determination to no longer settle for second-rate material, and the pair set about trying to find a project in which they could co-star. Both Sandra and Hugh were veterans of romantic comedies and, as Hugh's trepidation regarding the early drafts of *Bridget Jones's Diary* showed, they had very firm ideas as to what was required to create a worthwhile entry in the genre.

He claims he turned down the vast majority of scripts he was offered because the writing was terrible – they might have been romantic but they were not funny. After years of rejecting pitches, things finally fell into place when Sandra was finishing work on *Miss Congeniality*, a comedy in which she played a slobbish FBI agent forced to work undercover at a beauty pageant. The movie marked the directorial debut of writer Marc Lawrence, who had also worked with Sandra on *Forces of Nature*, another romantic comedy, this time co-starring Ben Affleck. While slaving away in the dubbing suite re-recording dialogue for *Miss Congeniality*, conversation moved on to Sandra's desire to find a project for her and Hugh to work on together, and Marc Lawrence promised to write one especially designed for the unique comedic talents of both stars. "Sandy and I had talked about it and she had been looking to work with Hugh for a long time," Marc confessed.

The script that he came up with was a deliberate throwback to the fast-talking 'battle of the sexes' comedies from the Forties, purposefully playing on Hugh's reputation as the modern embodiment of actors like Cary Grant, and tipping the balance in the 'romantic comedy' equation to favour the humour over the romance.

Sandra would play the role of Lucy Kelson, a brilliant but idealistic attorney who turns her back on the lucrative side of her profession to champion noble causes, such as saving her local community centre from demolition. Hugh would play George Wade, the charmingly scatter-brained millionaire whose company is behind the demolition project. A richer and more naïve version of *About A Boy's* Will, George was another self-absorbed fool, delegating most business decisions to his callous brother, though his innocently blinkered life view resulted in something slightly more pathetic, and less scathing than Will's isolated worldview. The two come to an agreement – Lucy will bring her legal prowess to work for Wade, and he'll get his company to leave her community centre alone. Needless to say, the dithering George soon comes to

HAIR TODAY...

rely on Lucy for every facet of his life – from office matters to choosing his tie, calling her at all hours with the most insignificant requests. Through their bickering and frustrations, the two – inevitably – find common ground and are faced with the question of if it's ever too late to say: "I love you".

Finally working together, the shoot was characterised by Hugh and Sandra cracking each other up and playing pranks on each other. Sandra took to leaving gift boxes in Hugh's trailer if he went away for the weekend, containing chocolates, wet wipes and condoms. "Doing this film was unbelievable," Hugh said on the *Live with Regis and Kelly* talk show. "I'm such a grumpy, neurotic, unpleasant actor normally on the film sets. She actually relaxed me and made me enjoy myself." The movie was also similar to *Extreme Measures* and *Mickey Blue Eyes*, in that Hugh was working closely with the producer – though this time it was co-star Sandra Bullock calling the shots, rather than Liz Hurley. It was at Sandra's insistence that the movie was shot on location in New York (the first to do so after the World Trade Center attacks) rather than using the usual Hollywood money-saving trick of dressing Canadian streets to pass for American cities. Sandra's love of New York's

HAIR TODAY...

architecture played a large part in the movie, and the threatened community centre was "played" in the movie by one of the cities listed landmark buildings – a Coney Island church that began life as the famous Childs Restaurant.

Hugh and Sandra's close friendship – and their easy, flirtatious banter during numerous shared press interviews for the film – inevitably led to rumours that they were dating or even, in particularly extreme cases, planning to marry! Even while shooting, the press were speculating that they were more than friends. Hugh and Sandra merely fuelled the fires by joking about it even more, a sign that Hugh had perhaps come to a realisation that it was more fun to bait the tabloids than to battle them. The crew of the film even got in on the joke, wearing signs pinned to their backs proclaiming "Hugh hates Sandy" or "Hugh loves Sandy" aimed at the photographers lurking for a snap of the celebrity pals.

Two Weeks Notice opened just in time for Christmas 2002 in America, against the second of the *Lord of the Rings* trilogy, *The Two Towers*. In what Hollywood marketeers like to call "counter-programming", those who weren't enticed by orcs and hobbits found a perfect alternative in the

HAIR TODAY...

winningly old-fashioned comedy romp, with both a charming love story and plenty of zinging one-liners. The UK release was held back until February, just in time for Valentine's day, and repeated its success. Despite surprisingly luke-warm reviews – "affable but undernourished" claimed *Variety*, the film industry trade magazine – *Two Weeks Notice* pulled in over $100 million, making it a sizeable hit.

11

More Hugh... actually

MORE HUGH... ACTUALLY

Having mentioned retiring from acting many times in interviews, from 2002 onwards there was a noticeable slowdown in Hugh's acting projects. Having been burned by promising scripts that translated into disappointing movies, and by less than successful ventures outside of the light comedy field, this period seemed to find Hugh accepting his niche in the Hollywood firmament, and opting to stick to the people he knew could deliver.

This, of course, meant Richard Curtis – who had written the scripts which had propelled Hugh to stardom in *Four Weddings* and cemented his reputation in *Notting Hill*. Curtis was planning to finally take the directors chair for a self-penned movie, something he hoped would be "the ultimate romantic comedy". With ten overlapping tales of love and loss in London during the build-up to Christmas, it was an ambitious undertaking and, naturally, the call went around the cream of Britain's thesping talent to fill out the sprawling cast. Old friends and co-stars of Hugh's signed up, such as Alan Rickman, Rowan Atkinson and Colin Firth, as well as other highly regarded actors like Liam Neeson. Hugh was signed on to play the new British Prime Minister, a bachelor who finds himself distracted from matters of state by the attractive girl who brings his tea and biscuits. Emma Thompson, making her fourth movie with Hugh, was on-board as the Prime Minister's sister, who has her own romantic problems to deal with.

The working title for the movie was *Love Actually Is All Around*, eventually chopped down to a more manageable *Love Actually*. The title still reflected Richard Curtis' intent though – this wasn't just to be a frothy romantic comedy, but a look at love in all its forms, from falling in

MORE HUGH... ACTUALLY

love, falling out of love, being in love and the love of family and friends. In a cynical time, it was a shamelessly optimistic ideal. "I thought it might be too girlie for a lot of blokes," Hugh admitted on Oprah. "When I was watching the preview in England, I thought, 'The guys are going to throw up'. But oddly enough, at the end, they liked it even more than the girls." As with *Notting Hill*, Curtis drew heavily on his own experiences for the situations in the movie. Colin Firth's storyline, for instance, saw him retreating to France to get over a recent break-up and finish his novel. While there, he finds himself falling for his Portuguese housekeeper despite not understanding a word she says. The set-up was taken from Curtis' own time in France (albeit with his girlfriend) and his awkwardness at driving their housekeeper home without being able to speak to her. He also poked fun at the success of his previous movies by having Bill Nighy's fading rockstar recording a horrible festive cover version of *Love Is All Around*, the song which had dominated the charts thanks to *Four Weddings*.

Of all the intermingled storylines, Hugh's was perhaps the most traditional – the sort of

MORE HUGH... ACTUALLY

sweet tale that ten years previously might have been a movie in it's own right. A Cinderella fable in which Hugh's typically amiable Prime Minister gains the strength to stand his political ground thanks to the example set by the tea girl, and, after some token soul-searching, throws decorum to the wind and admits his love for her, whisking her off her feet at – of all places – a local school concert. Never one for in-depth method acting, Hugh still felt he should try and get a feel for life as Prime Minister. Unfortunately, his only brush with the top job in Britain hadn't gone terribly well. During John Major's time as Prime Minister, Hugh had been invited to Number 10 for a drinks reception for people in the arts. "I think I had a few too many drinks", he confessed to Jay Leno on *The Tonight Show*, "and when John Major made a very funny speech to us all, I went up to him afterwards and said 'You know, the thing is, you're very funny and yet you're so boring on the television'. He was furious. I've never really been welcomed back."

With Curtis at the helm, the part of a rather more personable PM fitted Hugh like a hand-crafted suit, and offered endless opportunities to show off that winning charm. Curtis had also included a scene in which Hugh's character, finding himself alone, turns up the radio and dances around 10 Downing Street. The idea of the Prime Minister miming to pop songs in private was a funny one, but Hugh was less than ecstatic at the prospect. "It's just one of those unactable things like blushing," he admitted on US television's *The Charlie Rose Show*. "You just can't do it on camera. And I did dread it more than anything in the whole world, but he made me do it."

"I maintain to this day", Hugh continued jokingly, "that this is, in fact, the worst scene in the film, and the worst scene in any film ever."

For a movie with such a large star-studded cast, *Love Actually* was budgeted at a remarkably slender £30 million. Opening for Christmas 2003 (once again offering a mushy alternative to the fantasy battles of *Lord of the Rings*, this time the trilogy finale, *Return of the King*) it brought in just shy of $60 million at the US box office, making it healthily profitable, but not quite the result expected from such a cast. However, worldwide audiences were rather more receptive, bumping it up to $185 million, comfortably in the same bracket as the holy

MORE HUGH... ACTUALLY

trinity of *Four Weddings*, *Notting Hill* and *Bridget Jones's Diary*.

The ultimate romantic comedy actor had found his place in the ultimate romantic comedy. But where next?

12

Shy and retiring?

HUGH GRANT

SHY AND RETIRING?

What does the future hold for the star that has repeatedly claimed to have stumbled into acting, and never stumbled out?

Most immediately is the sequel to *Bridget Jones's Diary*, subtitled *Edge of Reason*. Hugh reprises his role as the heartless Daniel Cleaver in the continuation of Bridget's adventures now that she has finally landed her supposedly perfect man, Mark Darcy (Colin Firth again). The book pits the plucky lass against such modern-day obstacles as predatory boyfriend-stealing minxes (with "thighs like a baby giraffe"), useless builders and creepy bosses who insist you undertake the

SHY AND RETIRING?

most demeaning jobs. There's also the small matter of discovering what life is like when your perfect man is part of your life 24–7, votes Conservative and doesn't even do the washing up. Maybe the ruthless charm of Hugh wasn't such a bum deal after all?

Beyond that, Hugh is in no rush to sign up for another movie it seems. While promoting *Love Actually*, he admitted that he felt scared at the prospect of doing really big films and is not sure that he has the personality to enjoy trying to open a film at thousands of cinemas across the world with people interested only in how much money it makes that weekend. Although he is nervous of throwing away everything he has achieved in the last decade, Hugh believes that it might be the only thing for him, but he has no clear ideas of what might happen in the future.

That would put an end to persistent rumours that, despite their split, Hugh and Liz might reunite on-screen for a proposed remake of *The Cannonball Run* playing – with appropriate irony – a bickering married couple. The remake, which was first suggested in 2001, was planned to centre around another trans-American race – but with planes replacing cars. Burt Reynolds was

SHY AND RETIRING?

rumoured to return to the franchise, with people like Tim Allen and Pamela Anderson added to the otherwise new cast. John McTiernan, director of *Die Hard*, was supposedly lined up to direct but – as with so many Hollywood projects – it seems to have vanished into the ether.

Also falling by the wayside was *Wimbledon*, a comedy about a struggling tennis pro who finds inspiration and (of course) love with a controversial 'bad girl' player. Originally planned as a vehicle for Hugh and Cameron Diaz, the movie eventually went before cameras with *Master & Commander* star Paul Bettany and *Spider-Man's* Kirsten Dunst.

If the film world loses its lustre, Hugh has often hinted at writing as an alternative career to acting. During the lean years before Four Weddings, he even began a novel – still unfinished – called *Slack*, which he described to *Heat* magazine as "about what happens to time and personality and the warping effect it has when there is nothing to fill your life".

A life behind the camera might be on the cards also. When asked by *MovieMaker* magazine about his back-up plan should acting fame ever elude him again he told them: "I'd just have to jolly

SHY AND RETIRING?

well get up, find some drive and go back to writing my own stuff. I'd only direct or produce my own stuff. I'm not into anyone else's."

Off-screen Hugh and Liz remain close friends, and Hugh is the godfather to her son, Damian, having supported Liz during her very public break-up with millionaire Steve Bing. In 2003 Liz helped Hugh find a new home outside London (where he maintains his bachelor apartment), finally settling on the five-bedroomed Melksham Court, Gloucestershire, for a mere £3.2 million. The medieval mansion is only a few miles from Liz's equally lavish estate.

With Liz apparently set to marry her new love, Arun Nayar, Hugh has always insisted that he and Liz will never get back together. "She's with another guy and, you know, we're good friends," he said. "That train has sailed, as Austin Powers would say."

Now in his 40s, the prospect of marriage and children may be starting to appeal to Hugh. For someone who confessed while promoting *About A Boy* that he "doesn't know what the hell he's doing around children," the parenting urge may have finally caught up with him. "I need to get married and have children", he said. "Put it this way, if I

SHY AND RETIRING?

went to a party tonight and bumped into a fantastic girl – whereas three years ago it might have led to a short-term relationship – now I definitely keep my thoughts open to the idea of settling down and breeding. Definitely."

13

Filmography

HUGH GRANT

FILMOGRAPHY

FILM

Love Actually (2003):
The Prime Minister

Two Weeks Notice (2002):
George Wade

About a Boy (2002):
Will

Bridget Jones's Diary (2001):
Daniel Cleaver

Small Time Crooks (2000):
David Grant

Mickey Blue Eyes (1999):
Michael Felgate

Notting Hill (1999):
William Thacker

Extreme Measures (1996):
Dr. Guy Luthan

Restoration (1995):
Elias Finn

Sense and Sensibility (1995):
Edward Ferrars

Nine Months (1995):
Samuel 'Sam' Faulkner

The Englishman Who Went Up a Hill But Came Down a Mountain, (1995):
Reginald Anson

HUGH GRANT

FILMOGRAPHY

An Awfully Big Adventure (1995):
Meredith Potter
Four Weddings and a Funeral (1994):
Charles (Wedding one)
Sirens (1994):
Anthony Campion
Night Train to Venice (1993):
Martin Gamil
The Remains of the Day (1993):
Cardinal
Bitter Moon (1992):
Nigel
Impromptu (1991):
Frederic Chopin
The Big Man (1990):
Gordon
The Dawning (1988):
Harry
Nocturnes (1988):
Chopin
Bengali Night (1988):
Allan
Remando al viento (1988):
Lord Byron
The Lair of the White Worm (1988):
Lord James D'Ampton

HUGH GRANT

FILMOGRAPHY

White Mischief (1987):
Hugh
Maurice (1987):
Clive Durham
Privileged (1982):
Lord Adrian (credited as Hughie Grant)

TV
Robbie the Reindeer in Legend of the Lost Tribe (2002) (USA)
Comic Relief: *Doctor Who and the Curse of Fatal Death* (1999):
The (Handsome) 12th Doctor
Hooves of Fire (1999):
(voice: US version): Blitzen
The Changeling (1994):
Alsemero
The Trials of Oz (1991):
Richard Neville
Our Sons (1991):
James

"Till We Meet Again" (1989):
Bruno de Lancel
Champagne Charlie (1989):
Charles Heidsieck

FILMOGRAPHY

The Lady and the Highwayman (1989):
Lord Lucius Vyne
Lord Elgin and Some Stones of No Value (1986):
William Hamilton/James
The Dream Lover (1986/II):
Robert Drover
"Ladies in Charge" (1986) TV Series
Apsley Cherry-Garrard
"The Last Place on Earth" (1985):
Apsley Cherry-Garrard
Jenny's War (1985):
Peter Baines
Honour, Profit & Pleasure (1985):
Burlington

BIOGRAPHIES

OTHER BOOKS IN THE SERIES

Also available in the series:

Jennifer Aniston

David Beckham

George Clooney

Billy Connolly

Robert De Niro

Michael Douglas

Michael Jackson

Nicole Kidman

Jennifer Lopez

Madonna

Brad Pitt

Shane Richie

Jonny Wilkinson

Robbie Williams

OTHER BOOKS IN THE SERIES

JENNIFER ANISTON

She's been a Friend to countless millions worldwide, and overcame numerous hurdles to rise to the very top of her field. From a shy girl with a dream of being a famous actress, through being reduced to painting scenery for high school plays, appearing in a series of flop TV shows and one rather bad movie, Jennifer Aniston has persevered, finally finding success at the very top of the TV tree.

Bringing the same determination that got her a part on the world's best-loved TV series to her attempts at a film career, she's also worked her way from rom-com cutie up to serious, respected actress and box office draw, intelligently combining indie, cult and comedy movies into a blossoming career which looks set to shoot her to the heights of Hollywood's A-list. She's also found love with one of the world's most desirable men. Is Jennifer Aniston the ultimate Hollywood Renaissance woman? It would seem she's got more than a shot at such a title, as indeed, she seems to have it all, even if things weren't always that way. Learn all about Aniston's rise to fame in this compelling biography.

OTHER BOOKS IN THE SERIES

DAVID BECKHAM

This book covers the amazing life of the boy from East London who has not only become a world class footballer and the captain of England, but also an idol to millions, and probably the most famous man in Britain.

His biography tracks his journey, from the playing fields of Chingford to the Bernabau. It examines how he joined his beloved Manchester United and became part of a golden generation of talent that led to United winning trophies galore.

Beckham's parallel personal life is also examined, as he moved from tongue-tied football-obsessed kid to suitor of a Spice Girl, to one half of Posh & Becks, the most famous celebrity couple in Britain – perhaps the world. His non-footballing activities, his personal indulgences and changing styles have invited criticism, and even abuse, but his football talent has confounded the critics, again and again.

The biography looks at his rise to fame and his relationship with Posh, as well as his decision to leave Manchester for Madrid. Has it affected his relationship with Posh? What will the latest controversy over his sex life mean for celebrity's royal couple? And will he come back to play in England again?

OTHER BOOKS IN THE SERIES

GEORGE CLOONEY

The tale of George Clooney's astonishing career is an epic every bit as riveting as one of his blockbuster movies. It's a story of tenacity and determination, of fame and infamy, a story of succeeding on your own terms regardless of the risks. It's also a story of emergency rooms, batsuits, tidal waves and killer tomatoes, but let's not get ahead of ourselves.

Born into a family that, by Sixties' Kentucky standards, was dripping with show business glamour, George grew up seeing the hard work and heartache that accompanied a life in the media spotlight.

By the time stardom came knocking for George Clooney, it found a level-headed and mature actor ready and willing to embrace the limelight, while still indulging a lifelong love of partying and practical jokes. A staunchly loyal friend and son, a bachelor with a taste for the high life, a vocal activist for the things he believes and a born and bred gentleman; through failed sitcoms and blockbuster disasters, through artistic credibility and box office success, George Clooney has remained all of these things...and much, much more. Prepare to meet Hollywood's most fascinating megastar in this riveting biography.

OTHER BOOKS IN THE SERIES

BILLY CONNOLLY

In a 2003 London Comedy Poll to find Britain's favourite comedian, Billy Connolly came out on top. It's more than just Billy Connolly's all-round comic genius that puts him head and shoulders above the rest. Connolly has also proved himself to be an accomplished actor with dozens of small and big screen roles to his name. In 2003, he could be seen in *The Last Samurai* with Tom Cruise.

Connolly has also cut the mustard in the USA, 'breaking' that market in a way that chart-topping pop groups since The Beatles and the Stones have invariably failed to do, let alone mere stand-up comedians. Of course, like The Beatles and the Stones, Billy Connolly has been to the top of the pop charts too with D.I.V.O.R.C.E. in 1975.

On the way he's experienced heartache of his own with a difficult childhood and a divorce of his own, found the time and energy to bring up five children, been hounded by the press on more than one occasion, and faced up to some considerable inner demons. But Billy Connolly is a survivor. Now in his 60s, he's been in show business for all of 40 years, and 2004 finds him still touring. This exciting biography tells the story an extraordinary entertainer.

OTHER BOOKS IN THE SERIES

ROBERT DE NIRO

Robert De Niro is cinema's greatest chameleon. Snarling one minute, smirking the next, he's straddled Hollywood for a quarter of a century, making his name as a serious character actor, in roles ranging from psychotic taxi drivers to hardened mobsters. The scowls and pent-up violence may have won De Niro early acclaim but, ingeniously, he's now playing them for laughs, poking fun at the tough guy image he so carefully cultivated. Ever the perfectionist, De Niro holds nothing back on screen, but in real life he is a very private man – he thinks of himself as just another guy doing a job. Some job, some guy. There's more to the man than just movies. De Niro helped New York pick itself up after the September 11 terrorist attacks on the Twin Towers by launching the TriBeCa Film Festival and inviting everyone downtown. He runs several top-class restaurants and has dated some of the most beautiful women in the world, least of all supermodel Naomi Campbell. Now in his 60s, showered with awards and a living legend, De Niro's still got his foot on the pedal. There are six, yes six, films coming your way in 2004. In this latest biography, you'll discover all about his latest roles and the life of this extraordinary man.

OTHER BOOKS IN THE SERIES

MICHAEL DOUGLAS

Douglas may have been a shaggy-haired member of a hippy commune in the Sixties but just like all the best laidback, free-loving beatniks, he's gone on to blaze a formidable career, in both acting and producing.

In a career that has spanned nearly 40 years so far, Douglas has produced a multitude of hit movies including the classic *One Flew Over The Cuckoo's Nest* and *The China Syndrome* through to box office smashes such as *Starman* and *Face/Off*.

His acting career has been equally successful – from *Romancing The Stone* to *Wall Street* to *Fatal Attraction*, Douglas's roles have shown that he isn't afraid of putting himself on the line when up there on the big screen.

His relationship with his father; his stay in a top clinic to combat his drinking problem; the breakdown of his first marriage; and his publicised clash with the British media have all compounded to create the image of a man who's transformed himself from being the son of Hollywood legend Kirk Douglas, into Kirk Douglas being the dad of Hollywood legend, Michael Douglas.

OTHER BOOKS IN THE SERIES

MICHAEL JACKSON

Friday 29 August 1958 was not a special day in Gary, Indiana, and indeed Gary, was far from being a special place. But it was on this day and in this location that the world's greatest entertainer was to be born, Michael Joseph Jackson.

The impact that this boy was destined to have on the world of entertainment could never have been estimated. Here we celebrate Michael Jackson's extraordinary talents, and plot the defining events over his 40-year career. This biography explores the man behind the myth, and gives an understanding of what drives this special entertainer.

In 1993, there was an event that was to rock Jackson's world. His friendship with a 12-year-old boy and the subsequent allegations resulted in a lawsuit, a fall in record sales and a long road to recovery. Two marriages, three children and 10 years later there is a feeling of déjà vu as Jackson again deals with more controversy. Without doubt, 2004 proves to be the most important year in the singer's life. Whatever that future holds for Jackson, his past is secured, there has never been and there will never again be anything quite like Michael Jackson.

OTHER BOOKS IN THE SERIES

NICOLE KIDMAN

On 23 March 2003 Nicole Kidman won the Oscar for Best Actress for her role as Virginia Woolf in *The Hours*. That was the night that marked Nicole Kidman's acceptance into the upper echelons of Hollywood royalty. She had certainly come a long way from the 'girlfriend' roles she played when she first arrived in Hollywood – in films such as *Billy Bathgate* and *Batman Forever* – although even then she managed to inject her 'pretty girl' roles with an edge that made her acting stand out. And she was never merely content to be Mrs Cruise, movie star's wife. Although she stood dutifully behind her then husband in 1993 when he was given his star on the Hollywood Walk of Fame, Nicole got a star of her own 10 years later, in 2003.

Not only does Nicole Kidman have stunning good looks and great pulling power at the box office, she also has artistic credibility. But Nicole has earned the respect of her colleagues, working hard and turning in moving performances from a very early age. Although she dropped out of school at 16, no one doubts the intelligence and passion that are behind the fiery redhead's acting career, which includes television and stage work, as well as films. Find out how Kidman became one of Hollywood's most respected actresses in this compelling biography.

OTHER BOOKS IN THE SERIES

JENNIFER LOPEZ

There was no suggestion that the Jennifer Lopez of the early Nineties would become the accomplished actress, singer and icon that she is today. Back then she was a dancer on the popular comedy show *In Living Color* – one of the Fly Girls, the accompaniment, not the main event. In the early days she truly was Jenny from the block; the Bronx native of Puerto Rican descent – another hopeful from the east coast pursuing her dreams in the west.

Today, with two marriages under her belt, three multi-platinum selling albums behind her and an Oscar-winning hunk as one of her ex-boyfriends, she is one of the most talked about celebrities of the day. Jennifer Lopez is one of the most celebrated Hispanic actresses of all time.

Her beauty, body and famous behind, are lusted after by men and envied by women throughout the world. She has proven that she can sing, dance and act. Yet her critics dismiss her as a diva without talent. And the criticisms are not just about her work, some of them are personal. But what is the reality? Who is Jennifer Lopez, where did she come from and how did get to where she is now? This biography aims to separate fact from fiction to reveal the real Jennifer Lopez.

OTHER BOOKS IN THE SERIES

MADONNA

Everyone thought they had Madonna figured out in early 2003. The former Material Girl had become Maternal Girl, giving up on causing controversy to look after her two children and set up home in England with husband Guy Ritchie. The former wild child had settled down and become respectable. The new Madonna would not do anything to shock the establishment anymore, she'd never do something like snogging both Britney Spears and Christina Aguilera at the MTV Video Music Awards... or would she?

Of course she would. Madonna has been constantly reinventing herself since she was a child, and her ability to shock even those who think they know better is both a tribute to her business skills and the reason behind her staying power. Only Madonna could create gossip with two of the current crop of pop princesses in August and then launch a children's book in September. In fact, only Madonna would even try.

In her 20-year career she has not just been a successful pop singer, she is also a movie star, a business woman, a stage actress, an author and a mother. Find out all about this extraordinary modern-day icon in this new compelling biography.

OTHER BOOKS IN THE SERIES

BRAD PITT

From the launch pad that was his scene stealing turn in *Thelma And Louise* as the sexual-enlightening bad boy. To his character-driven performances in dramas such as *Legends of the Fall* through to his Oscar-nominated work in *Twelve Monkeys* and the dark and razor-edged Tyler Durden in *Fight Club*, Pitt has never rested on his laurels. Or his good looks.

And the fact that his love life has garnered headlines all over the world hasn't hindered Brad Pitt's profile away from the screen either – linked by the press to many women, his relationships with the likes of Juliette Lewis and Gwyneth Paltrow. Then of course, in 2000, we had the Hollywood fairytale ending when he tied the silk knot with Jennifer Aniston.

Pitt's impressive track record as a superstar, sex symbol *and* credible actor looks set to continue as he has three films lined up for release over the next year – as Achilles in the Wolfgang Peterson-helmed Troy; Rusty Ryan in the sequel *Ocean's Twelve* and the titular Mr Smith in the thriller *Mr & Mrs Smith* alongside Angelina Jolie. Pitt's ever-growing success shows no signs of abating. Discover all about Pitt's meteoric rise from rags to riches in this riveting biography.

OTHER BOOKS IN THE SERIES

SHANE RICHIE

Few would begrudge the current success of 40-year-old Shane Richie. To get where he is today, Shane has had a rather bumpy roller coaster ride that has seen the hard working son of poor Irish immigrants endure more than his fair share of highs and lows – financially, professionally and personally.

In the space of four decades he has amused audiences at school plays, realised his childhood dream of becoming a Pontins holiday camp entertainer, experienced homelessness, beat his battle with drink, became a million-aire then lost the lot. He's worked hard and played hard.

When the producers of *EastEnders* auditioned Shane for a role in the top TV soap, they decided not to give him the part, but to create a new character especially for him. That character was Alfie Moon, manager of the Queen Vic pub, and very quickly Shane's TV alter ego has become one of the most popular soap characters in Britain. This biography is the story of a boy who had big dreams and never gave up on turning those dreams into reality

OTHER BOOKS IN THE SERIES

JONNY WILKINSON

"There's 35 seconds to go, this is the one. It's coming back for Jonny Wilkinson. He drops for World Cup glory. It's over! He's done it! Jonny Wilkinson is England's Hero yet again..."

That memorable winning drop kick united the nation, and lead to the start of unprecedented victory celebrations throughout the land. In the split seconds it took for the ball to leave his boot and slip through the posts, Wilkinson's life was to change forever. It wasn't until three days later, when the squad flew back to Heathrow and were met with a rapturous reception, that the enormity of their win, began to sink in.

Like most overnight success stories, Wilkinson's journey has been a long and dedicated one. He spent 16 years 'in rehearsal' before achieving his finest performance, in front of a global audience of 22 million, on that rainy evening in Telstra Stadium, Sydney.

But how did this modest self-effacing 24-year-old become England's new number one son? This biography follows Jonny's journey to international stardom. Find out how he caught the rugby bug, what and who his earliest influences were and what the future holds for our latest English sporting hero.

OTHER BOOKS IN THE SERIES

ROBBIE WILLIAMS

Professionally, things can't get much better for Robbie Williams. In 2002 he signed the largest record deal in UK history when he re-signed with EMI. The following year he performed to over 1.5 million fans on his European tour, breaking all attendance records at Knebworth with three consecutive sell-out gigs.

Since going solo Robbie Williams has achieved five number one hit singles, five number one hit albums; 10 Brits and three Ivor Novello awards. When he left the highly successful boy band Take That in 1995 his future seemed far from rosy. He got off to a shaky start. His nemesis, Gary Barlow, had already recorded two number one singles and the press had virtually written Williams off. But then in December 1997, he released his Christmas single, *Angels.*

Angels re-launched his career – it remained in the Top 10 for 11 weeks. Since then Robbie has gone from strength to strength, both as a singer and a natural showman. His live videos are a testament to his performing talent and his promotional videos are works of art.

This biography tells of Williams' journey to the top – stopping off on the way to take a look at his songs, his videos, his shows, his relationships, his rows, his record deals and his demons.